ANOTHER TITAN TRIUMPH!

HELIX
COMICS

HEROES

46 COMPLETE STORIES INSIDE!

VOLUME TWO

Uncle Burk's Fine Comics

CALL TOLL FREE
1-888-266-4226

ORDER QUANTITIES AND SAVE!

Lettering and design
by JG ROSHELL OF
COMICRAFT

Collected Edition
Dustjacket A by TIM
SALE & JG ROSHELL

Collected Edition
Dustjacket B by
GENE HA

Paintings by TIM SALE
and DAVE STEWART

Uncle Burk's Fine Comics

CALL TOLL FREE
1-888-COMIC-BOOK

**LOOKING FOR
LOWER PRICES?**

Special Thanks to

FRANK MASTROMAURO
and NANCI QUESADA

and the folks from
Helix Comics:

ARON ELI COLEITE
JOE POKASKI
JESSE ALEXANDER
JEPH LOEB
CHUCK KIM
MARK WARSHAW

HEROES Volume 2
published by WildStorm Productions
888 Prospect St. #240, La Jolla, CA 92037

Compilation, cover art, additional art Copyright ©
2009 Universal Studios Licensing LLLP. Heroes is
a trademark and copyright of NBC Studios, Inc. All
rights reserved. Originally published at www.nbc.
com/Heroes/novels © 2007, 2008, NBC Studios, Inc.

MAIL THIS COUPON TODAY!

DC Comics, a Warner Bros. Entertainment Company

OH... OH... I...

OHHHHH...

SOME OF THEM *SMILE.* HAVE YOU NOTICED?

AFTER THE INITIAL SHOCK, I MEAN. YOU CAN ALMOST SEE IT COME OVER THEM.

A WAVE ROLLING IN, FILLING THE EMPTY SPACES WITH... *STILLNESS. PEACE.*

MAKES SENSE. I'M SURE MR. PARKMAN HERE ISN'T THE ONLY ONE WHO'D WANT TO BE RELIEVED OF HIS BURDENS.

LOVE TO KNOW WHAT IT FEELS LIKE, JUST ONCE.

I WAS BEING RHETORICAL. I KNOW YOU SURE AS HELL AREN'T GOING TO TELL ME.

SOMETIMES, IT'S LIKE PICKING FLOWERS JUST AFTER A SPRING RAIN...

SOMETIMES, LIKE REACHING INTO THE MOIST SOIL OF FRESHLY DUG GRAVES. GRUBS BITING AT YOUR FINGERS...

"HAITI WAS DYING, STRANGLING IN THE GRIP OF THE DUVALIERS...

"YET, JUST TWENTY-FIVE MILES OUT OF PORT-AU-PRINCE... MY VILLAGE WAS UNTOUCHED.

"MOST SAID THAT WE LIVED UNDER THE PROTECTION OF THE OLD WAYS. TRUE BELIEVERS AND HONORED SERVANTS OF THE LOA...

"BUT MANY COUNTRYMEN HAD DIED SCREAMING WITH THE NAMES OF THE OLD ONES ON THEIR TONGUES... IT WAS NOT JUST FAITH...

"IT WAS MY FATHER.

"THE HOUNGAN. THE PRIEST. MY FATHER WAS *SPECIAL*.

"IT WAS WHISPERED AROUND OUR VILLAGE THAT MANY HAD BEEN CHOSEN BY THE LOA FOR SACRIFICE AND GRACE...

"...BUT GUILLAME WAS THE ONLY HOUNGAN WHOM THEY TRULY LOVED.

"THOUGH NO ONE, GOD OR MAN, COULD HAVE LOVED HIM MORE THAN I DID."

BOY. I'M HUNGRY.

HE SHOULD BE PRESIDENT OF HAITI! PRESIDENT OF THE U.S.!

ARE YOU GOING TO TALK ABOUT MY FATHER ALL DAY? YOU'LL SCARE THE FISH.

HOW CAN YOU BE LIKE THAT? YOU'VE SEEN OTHER HOUNGUN...

THAT FAT MOLO IN PIERRE JUST SPITS AND SHAKES AND WOMEN LAUGH AT HIM....BUT YOUR FATHER...

REAL POWERS. ADMIT IT. YOU KNOW HE'S SPECIAL.

YES. HE IS.

KRAKK

WH- WHAT WAS THAT?

"TONTON MACOUTES."

9

"TONTON MACOUTES. THE 'BOOGEYMEN.'"

"DUVALIER'S PRIVATE MILITIA. MURDERERS. RAPISTS. TORTURERS. MONSTERS IN HUMAN SKINS."

I'LL ASK AGAIN. WHERE IS THE ONE CALLED GUILLAME?

OR DO I MOVE FROM PIGS ON FOUR LEGS...TO PIGS ON TWO?

"IT WAS COMMON FOR THE TONTON MACOUTES TO COME FOR POPULAR LEADERS LIKE MY FATHER..."

NO! GUILLAME, THEY'LL--

I WALK WITH LEGBA AND OGUN. I LAY WITH SAMARA AND DELUN...

"...BUT NEVER MY VILLAGE. MY FATHER NEVER LET THEM GET CLOSE ENOUGH."

I AM BLISS AND I AM HORROR AND YOU, MY FRIEND...

...HAVE MADE A TERRIBLE MISTAKE.

I...GUH... M-MOTHER ...?

GLARRRGH

≡NNNNGH≡

"BLISS AND HORROR. MY FATHER'S TOOLS. MY FATHER'S GIFT."

FATHER!!

"BUT IMAGINE *HIS* HORROR... WHEN THOSE GIFTS FAILED HIM...

?

"...BECAUSE OF *ME*."

PLAY *TRICKS* ON ME?!

YOU...WHAT DID YOU *DO* TO ME?!

WHAT DID YOU DO?!

IT TAKES A VILLAGE

"IT HAD BEEN ALMOST TWENTY-FOUR HOURS SINCE THE 'BOOGEYMEN' LEFT...

"...SINCE MY FATHER'S POWER FAILED OUR VILLAGE, AND THE TONTON MACOUTES DID AS THEY PLEASED WITH OUR GOODS, OUR MONEY, OUR WOMEN.

"TWENTY FOUR HOURS SINCE THEY HUNG HIM UP LIKE MEAT, AND NO MAN, WOMAN...OR CHILD HAD MOVED TO CUT HIM DOWN.

"NOT EVEN HIS OWN SON.

"THIS WAS HIS PUNISHMENT FOR FAILING TO PROTECT US. FOR 'BETRAYING THE LOA'...

"SAVAGE AS THE ATTACK ON MY VILLAGE AND MY FATHER HAD BEEN...ONLY ONE THING ABOUT THAT DAY STILL CHILLS MY BLOOD...

"...THE WAY HE LOOKED AT ME.

JOE KELLY OF
MAN OF ACTION STUDIOS
Story

STAZ JOHNSON *Art*

CHRIS SOTOMAYOR *Colors*

COMICRAFT *Lettering*

13

14

REST NOW, BOY. TILL DAWN. WHEN THE VEIL BETWEEN WORLDS IS THINNEST.

THEN WHAT?

...

DO YOU HATE ME?

...

WE TELL A STORY, OF THE SERPENT AND THE CRANE.

THE SERPENT WAS A CREATURE OF AMBITION, TIRED OF CRAWLING ON HIS BELLY AND EATING GRUBS AND MICE.

ONE DAY, HE SPOTTED THE CRANE. CAREFREE. STUPID. BUT SHE COULD *FLY*. THE SUN SHONE ON HER ALWAYS. SHE SLEPT IN CLOUDS. DRANK FROM RAINBOWS.

"*WHAT A WASTE,*" THOUGHT THE SNAKE. "*IF I COULD FLY, THE THINGS I COULD ACCOMPLISH!*"

SO ONE DAY, HE FOUND THE WATERING HOLE WHERE THE CRANE DEIGNED TO BATHE...

AND SWALLOWED HER WHOLE.

HE TOOK HER WINGS, AND MADE THEM HIS OWN. AND HE FLEW.

HE FLEW AROUND THE SUN. HE FLEW TO THE MOON. HE ATE THE CLOUDS AND PLAYED IN THE RAIN.

ISN'T THAT GOOD? THAT HE GOT WHAT HE WANTED?

YES. VERY GOOD. VERY IMPORTANT...

BUT WHAT GOOD IS IT TO FLY, IF YOU HAVE NOWHERE TO GO? ONCE HE HAD THE POWER, THE SNAKE LOST TOUCH WITH THE GROUND.

WHEN THE LOA MOUNT ME, I HAVE *POWER*. I COULD DRIVE MEN TO *ECSTACY* OR *HORROR*.

I COULD *LEAD*, MOVE *NATIONS*...

...INSTEAD, I GET THEM HIGH AND I SLEEP WITH THEIR WOMEN.

I HAVE FORGOTTEN THE GROUND, AND MUST MAKE PENANCE FOR IT.

"WHEN I FINALLY DID SLEEP THAT NIGHT, I DREAMT ONLY OF SNAKES WITH NO TEETH, AND A CRANE WITH A BROKEN NECK.

"MY FATHER HAD ALWAYS BEEN A MAN OF PASSION. IT WAS WHAT MADE HIM SUCH A POWERFUL HOUNGAN."

"THAT DAY, AT THE TOP OF THE WORLD, WHERE THE REALM OF SPIRITS AND WORLD OF MAN MET IN BLOOD AND SHADOW..."

"...HE WAS AS PASSIONATE ABOUT KILLING HIS ONLY SON AS I HAD EVER SEEN HIM. MORE SO."

IT TAKES A VILLAGE

Part 4 of 4

JOE KELLY OF MAN OF ACTION STUDIOS
Story

STAZ JOHNSON
Art

EDGAR AT STUDIO F *Colors*
COMICRAFT *Lettering*

I FORGIVE YOU, BOY. KNOW THAT. I FORGIVE YOU FOR WHAT YOU ARE...

...SO YOU WILL NOT SUFFER.

"AND THAT PASSION HAD BEEN REWARDED. MY FATHER'S POWERS HAD RETURNED."

FATHER... NO... PLEASE...

"I KNEW NOTHING THEN OF GENETICS, OF BIO-CHEMICAL ABERRANCE.

"OR HOW SHAME COULD CRIPPLE *MY OWN* ABILITIES...

"I KNEW ONLY THAT THE 'DEITY' WHOM I ADMIRED WITH EVERYTHING...HAD CALLED ME A POISON.

"THAT THE LOA WHO COMMAND THE WORLD TOLD HIM I WAS A CANCER THAT HAD TO BE REMOVED FOR TRANSCENDENCE...

"AND IF MY DEATH WOULD HEAL HIM... GIVE HIM PEACE...

"...I WOULD DIE FOR HIM. WITH PRIDE.

"BUT I WAS STILL A BOY... AND I COULD NOT LEAVE MY FATHER WITHOUT ONE LAST TOUCH.

"I BECAME ONE WITH MY FATHER'S MIND, AND FOR THE FIRST TIME, SAW HIM -- NOT AS A GOD, OR A PRIEST...

"...BUT AS A *MAN*.

"A MAN WHO LOVED HIS SON, THOUGH IT DID NOT SHOW FOR FEAR IT WOULD MAKE HIM LOOK WEAK...

"MEMORIES, MOMENTS, HIDDEN LIKE JEWELS SCATTERED IN A MUDDY FIELD. BUT I COULD *FIND THEM*.

"I COULD FIND THEM AND *SHOW THEM* TO HIM, IN ALL OF THEIR RADIANCE."

I... OH... BOY...

SON.

I HAVE FORGOTTEN THE GROUND. I HAVE FORGOTTEN.

"THAT DAY, MY FATHER *'REMEMBERED THE GROUND'*... AND HE FLEW...

"BUT NOT IN THE WAY EITHER OF US EXPECTED.

"HE LEFT ME WITH THE NECKLACE, THE SNAKE AND CRANE TO GUIDE ME...

"...AND A FINAL COMMAND...

Betty

Part 1 of 4

JOE CASEY OF
MAN OF ACTION STUDIOS
Story

RYAN ODAGAWA
Art

JOHN STARR
Colors

COMICRAFT
Lettering

NOT LONG AGO...

I HATE MY NAME.

I'D LOVE TO JUST CHANGE IT. GET A NEW ONE.

I HATE THIS PLACE. TOO MANY FAKES.

MOST OF THEM THINK THEY'RE BETTER THAN ME.

SEEMS LIKE IT'S *ALWAYS* BEEN THAT WAY...

...DID YOU SEE WHAT SHE WAS WEARING IN CHEM CLASS? *SO* LAST YEAR...!

NO DOUBT. BUT AT LEAST SHE'S GOT THE GHOST OF FASHION SENSE PAST...

...AND THERE'S *NO ESCAPE.*

HOW 'BOUT THAT *NEW GIRL*... WHAT'S HER NAME...?

BETTY SOMETHING...

OH, *TOTALLY!* Y'KNOW, SHE'S NOT THAT NEW, THOUGH. BEEN HERE SINCE LAST YEAR...

WHO CARES?! SHE'S COMPLETELY DISGUSTING.

HANGS WITH THE RESIN CROWD...

WHAT*EVER*... SHE'S IN SERIOUS NEED OF DIET AND EXERCISE.

EXTREME MAKEOVER REJECT...

...LOSER OF THE WORST KIND...

TOTAL BETTY... *THERE'S* THE NEW TERM FOR LOSER...

Mouse wuz here

"*BETTY*". SEE... THAT'S WHY I HATE MY NAME.

I HEARD A HILARIOUS RUMOR THAT SHE WANTED TO TRY OUT FOR THE SQUAD...

NO WAY!

I KNOW...CAN YOU IMAGINE?! A TOE TOUCH OR EVEN A HURDLER... OUCH.

THINK OF THE PYRAMID...

SHE JUST NEEDS TO BE PUT OUT OF HER MISERY. STRAIGHT TO THE GLUE FACTORY...

I WONDER IF THEY'D BE ANY DIFFERENT IF THEY KNEW I WAS HERE...

CHECK IT OUT --

-- READY! OKAY! WHAT'S FOR LUNCH?!

NO DOUBT. SOMEONE'S GOT SOME UNREALISTIC LIFE EXPECTATIONS...

YOU THINK SO, MISS PERFECT...?

SOME GIRLS'LL NEVER HANG. LAW OF THE JUNGLE, Y'KNOW.

SPEAKING OF WHICH, HOW LAME IS THE HOMECOMING DANCE THEME...?

BEYOND LAME. MISS PRICHER THINKS, Y'KNOW, IT'S GENIUS.

PRICHER'S LAME.

SO UNTOUCHABLE...

...YOU DON'T KNOW WHAT IT'S LIKE...

...TO BE SO...

STILL...THE KEGGER AFTERWARDS IS GOING TO...

...TO...

OMIGOD...!

WHAT THE HELL?!

AAHHHH...

...WHAT'S HAPPENING TO ME?!

AAAAHH!

IT'S ALL POINTLESS, ANYWAY...

... THESE STUPID SCHOOL RITUALS. PEP RALLIES. HOMECOMING DANCES. LIKE SHEEP LED TO THE SLAUGHTER.

MY FRIEND, *REN*, IS AS CLOSE AS IT GETS WHEN IT COMES TO *RELATABILITY*.

HE GETS IT.

I TAKE COMFORT IN MY FANTASY BLOODBATH SCENARIOS. THE POWER OF NEGATIVE THINKING...

YOU WANNA HIT CLANCY'S AFTER SIXTH PERIOD?

WHY WAIT? SO I CAN SIT THROUGH A.P. HISTORY OF WHITE AMERICA? BESIDES...

... IT BEATS HAVING TO WALK THE LUNCHROOM GAUNTLET YET AGAIN.

IT'S LIKE THIS EVERY DAY. WE'RE THE LUNCHTIME *FREAKSHOW*...

WATCH YER STEP, BURNOUT--!

HUUHHNN--!

YO... I GIVE IT AN *EIGHT.*

THANK YOU, THANK YOU... AS YOU CAN SEE, I HAVE MANY TALENTS BOTH ON AND OFF THE FIELD...

REN'S LEARNED HOW TO *BLOCK OUT* THE RAIN OF INSULTS. I HAVEN'T.

WELL, *THAT* SUCKED.

I KNEW IT'D BEEN TOO LONG SINCE I ENDURED SOME *PHYSICAL* ABUSE.

I REALLY *HATE* THOSE GUYS...

YOU AND ME BOTH. BUT, I JUST THINK OF THEIR *HOME LIFE* AND IT PUTS A SMILE ON MY FACE...

WHAT DO YOU *MEAN*...?

C'MON, DIDN'T YOU SEE *THE BREAKFAST CLUB?* THEY'RE ALL AFRAID OF THEIR DADDIES...

... THEY'RE SHAKIN' IN THEIR CLEATS WHEN THEY DON'T GET A TOUCHDOWN. THAT MEANS AN AUTOMATIC *BEATING* AT HOME.

AT LEAST... THAT'S WHAT *I'M* HOPING...

35

THE NEXT DAY.

YOU GUYS HEAR ABOUT *CRASH* --?!

HELL, YEAH, WE HEARD. I CAN'T FIGGER IT OUT, Y'KNOW...

...I MEAN, WE JUST SAW HIM IN THE LOCKER ROOM AFTER PRACTICE. NO BIG DEAL. HE HAD TO HANG BACK...

"... NEXT THING YOU KNOW, COACH FINDS HIM ON THE FLOOR, DROOLING LIKE A BABY.

"THEY SAID HIS MIND WAS TOTALLY *FRIED*. DOESN'T EVEN KNOW HIS OWN *NAME* ANYMORE. PSYCHO CITY..."

-- HEARD HE WAS *TOTALLY* COKED OUT --

...BRAIN DEAD...

...HEARD COACH MARBORO KICKED THE CRAP OUT OF HIM FOR GOING OUT OF BOUNDS ON A PLAY...

-- MENTAL INSTITUTION --

...COPS CAME DOWN...

...I'M TELLIN' YA, I HEARD CRASH OWED MONEY TO SOME MOB GUY...

C'MON, THAT AIN'T HAPPENING. WHAT *HAPPENED* WAS... CRASH HIT HIS HEAD IN THE LOCKER ROOM. SPLIT IT RIGHT OPEN. HELLO, BRAIN DAMAGE...

YOU HEARD THIS *CRASH* THING...?

WHAT, THAT HE'S A VEGETABLE? YEAH, I HEARD. LOTTA *RUMORS* GOING AROUND...

WELL, THIS ONE'S ABSOLUTELY *TRUE*. I OVERHEARD THE GUIDANCE COUNSELOR TALKING ABOUT IT. WHAT LITTLE MIND HE HAD... IS *GONE*.

TELL YOU WHAT... COULDN'T HAVE HAPPENED TO A MORE DESERVING DIRTBAG.

WHOEVER HAD THE MEANS TO SEND HIS SOUL INTO THE ABYSS HAS MY RESPECT, BIG TIME...

...I'M TALKIN' NATIONAL *HERO*.

MY HERO, ANYWAY.

I THINK I'M ON A ROLL.

LET'S SEE IF I CAN MAKE *THIS* WORK...

...I DUNNO... CRASH WAS *KINDA* CUTE. NOT *MATTHEW FOX* HOT, BUT NOT BAD...

HE ASKED ME TO HOMECOMING, Y'KNOW...

...I NEVER GAVE HIM AN ANSWER.

SO THIS IS THE *PLACE*, HUH...?

FUNNY THING ABOUT RUMORS...

...SO, I HEARD IT WAS SOME KIND OF PLANNED THING... TRENCHCOAT MAFIA-STYLE...

...YOU CAN'T EXACTLY *CONTROL* THEM.

... TOTAL CLASS WARFARE, I'M TELLIN' YA. CRASH WAS A *TARGET*, Y'KNOW...?

WHOA...!

THEY TAKE ON A LIFE OF THEIR OWN.

...THAT'S WHAT I *HEARD*--

I HEARD THAT, TOO. YOU WANNA FIND OUT *WHO*... YOU GOTTA DO, LIKE, A *USUAL SUSPECTS* THING...

RIGHT, RIGHT... WHO'S THE MOST OBVIOUS CANDIDATE...?

... PROCESS OF ELIMINATION. I'M SURPRISED THEY HAVEN'T *ARRESTED* HIM YET.

AND THEY'RE SURE IT'S *HIM*...?

...NO WAY. HOW'D HE DO IT?

WHO CARES? I ALWAYS *KNEW* HE WAS SOME KINDA *SATAN WORSHIPPER* OR SOMETHING...

DON'T MATTER HOW. CRASH WAS ONE OF US...

... AND IF THIS REN CHUCKER DID HIM IN, THEN IT'S *PAYBACK* TIME.

YOU GUYS KNOW WHAT I'M SAYIN'...?

40

Betty

Part 3 of 4

TRYING TO MINGLE WITH THE BEAUTIFUL PEOPLE...WHAT WAS I *THINKING*...?!

REN'S GOT IT RIGHT. HE'S JUST *HONEST* WITH HIMSELF. MORE THAN ANYONE I KNOW...

JOE CASEY OF **MAN OF ACTION STUDIOS**
Story

RYAN ODAGAWA
Art

JOHN STARR   **COMICRAFT**
Colors   *Lettering*

I WALKED RIGHT UP OUT OF CLASS WHEN THE TEACHER TOLD US...

...CAME STRAIGHT HERE. I CAN'T... BELIEVE WHAT THEY *DID* TO YOU. AND NO ONE KNOWS. THEY'RE DENYING *EVERYTHING*.

I HAVE TO *TELL* YOU SOMETHING, REN. I THINK... THIS IS *MY* FAULT.

I KNOW YOU DIDN'T HAVE ANYTHING TO DO WITH CRASH'S... WELL...WITH WHAT HAPPENED TO HIM.

KNOW IT FOR A FACT.

A FEW DAYS AGO... I FOUND OUT I COULD *DO* THINGS. MAKE PEOPLE *SEE* THINGS.

WHATEVER I *WANTED* THEM TO SEE.

I KNOW WHAT YOU'RE THINKING... BUT IT'S ABSOLUTELY TRUE. I WAS... Y'KNOW...REALLY *SCARED* AND *CONFUSED* AT FIRST.

BUT THEN I REALIZED... THE *POWER*...

I CAN TELL... YOU THINK I'M *NUTS*. BUT I MADE CRASH *SEE* SOMETHING... *EXPERIENCE* SOMETHING THAT SENT HIM OVER THE EDGE.

I CAN MAKE *ANYONE* THINK THEY'VE SEEN SOMETHING...

CHECK IT OUT...

44

...THE HOMECOMING *PEP RALLY* WILL BEGIN IN TEN MINUTES. ALL STUDENTS REPORT TO THE GYMNASIUM...

THEY ACT LIKE NOTHING REALLY HAPPENED.

ONE JOCK. ONE LOSER. NO BIG DEAL. LIKE THE SCALES ARE BALANCED OR SOMETHING.

THEY TALK ABOUT IT... THEY GOSSIP ABOUT IT... BUT NO ONE'S ACCOUNTABLE...

...I DUNNO, MAN... IT JUST LOOKS KINDA *BAD*, Y'KNOW...?

LISTEN... IT WAS JUST *PAYBACK*, THAT'S ALL...

... BUT WE SURE AS HELL DIDN'T BREAK ANY BONES OR THROW HIM DOWN THAT HILL. THAT WAS ALL *HIM*.

IS IT *OUR* FAULT HE BUYS IT IN THE HOSPITAL? THAT THE DOCTORS COULDN'T SAVE HIM?!

... ALL STUDENTS REPORT TO THE GYMNASIUM...

C'MON...FORGET ALL ABOUT THAT. WE'VE GOT A *PEP RALLY* GOIN' DOWN. PRIORITIES, RIGHT...?

ALRIGHT, ALRIGHT...

PRIORITIES. YOU GOTTA BE *KIDDING* ME.

I'VE GOT ME SOME NEW PRIORITIES NOW...

...SOME UNFINISHED BUSINESS.

NOOOOOOO--!

...?

IF ONLY IT WERE *REAL*...

HOLY... HELL...! DID YOU JUST SEE WHAT I SAW?!

I... I THINK SO...

OMIGOD... OMIGOD...

WHU... WHY DOES THIS KEEP *HAPPENING*...?!

WHO'S... WHO'S *DOING* THIS TO US?!

SO, WHATEVER. I'M DONE WITH THIS HELLHOLE.

MAYBE THEY WON'T SOON FORGET HOW *FRAGILE* THEY ARE...

...HOW FRAGILE WE *ALL* ARE.

AND NOW THAT I KNOW EXACTLY WHAT I'M *CAPABLE* OF, I SHOULD PUT IT TO SOME *USE*, RIGHT?

FIRST THINGS FIRST...

... ENOUGH OF POOR *BETTY*. TIME TO CHANGE THE GAME.

FROM NOW ON... THEY'LL ALL SEE WHAT I *WANT* THEM TO SEE...

SOMETIMES YOU JUST NEED THE RIGHT *NAME*... SOMETHING THAT SETS A TONE... SOMETHING THAT GOES WITH MY NEW *LOOK*...

CANDICE.

THAT'S A GOOD NAME.

JOE CASEY OF **MAN OF ACTION STUDIOS**
Story

RYAN ODAGAWA
Art

JOHN STARR
Colors

COMICRAFT
Lettering

End

GOLDEN HANDSHAKE
MAN OVERBOARD
Part **1** of *4*

17 YEARS AGO...

STATUS REPORT:
Location: Côte d'Azur.
The French Riviera.

Notes: Have tracked down extortionist and murderer *Rollo Fusor* --'special' whose ability to rapidly dehydrate water from whatever he touches has been used to bankrupt many in the European elite.

Considered a class 'A' priority by the higher-ups before he seemingly fell off the face of the planet seven years ago. Fusor was my partner Haram's first failed case. Haram wasn't about to let him get away again.

PU-KT PAK POKK

ƎNNGƐ DAMN IT! NOT *NOW!*

STEVEN T. SEAGLE & DUNCAN ROULEAU
OF **MAN OF ACTION STUDIOS** *Story*

MICHAEL GAYDOS
Art

CHRIS SOTOMAYOR *Colors*
COMICRAFT *Lettering*

ƎNNGƐ NOT NOW, NOT NOW, NOT NOW!

SON OF A--!

KLT
KLT
KLT
KLT

TEMPER, TEMPER, PARTNER...

YOU'VE *GOT* THIS. DON'T LET YOUR NERVES--

DON'T LECTURE ME, CLAUDE! I KNOW WHAT I'M *DOING.*

THEN ACCEPT HIS *OFFER.*

ACCEPT*?!* THERE'S NO *NEGOTIATING* WITH THIS LUNATIC!

FUSOR IS A *MONSTER!* HE SUCKS THE *LIFE* OUT OF HIS VICTIMS AND --

I'M *NOT* LETTIN' HIM GET AWAY. I GOT HIM DEAD TO RIGHTS THIS TIME, I'M --

GOING TO GET HIS *HOSTAGES* KILLED IF WE DON'T LET HIM *THINK* HE'S A FREE MAN.

THINK...?

ACCEPT HIS TERMS. WHEN HE RUNS...I'LL *STOP* HIM ON THE OTHER SIDE OF THE BOAT-HOUSE.

GOOD, 'CAUSE I'M *DONE.* THE ONLY THING ON THE OTHER SIDE OF THIS FOR *ME* IS *RETIREMENT.*

DON'T TALK CRAZY, HARAM. I DON'T WANT TO BREAK IN A NEW PARTNER.

IT'LL ALL WORK OUT IF YOU JUST *STICK WITH THE PLAN* THIS TIME.

FUSOR! YOU'VE GOT YOUR DEAL!

LET THE HOSTAGES GO!

NO TRICKS, ARAB! I HAVE EXPLOSIVES ON MONSIEUR PIZET AND HIS LOVELY LADY FRIEND HERE!

I SEE ANYONE FOLLOWING ME... "BOOM"!

MORE BLOOD ON YOUR PATHETIC HANDS!

DON'T WORRY FUSOR, YOU WON'T SEE A THING...

OH NO...

DON'T WORRY, FOLKS, YOU'RE GONNA BE OKAY --

I'VE GOT -- YOU --?

NO, NO, LOVE --

KLATCH

WE'VE GOT YOU.

WHAT THE --?!

CLAUDE --!

GOLDEN HANDSHAKE

Part **2** of 4 AN AMERICAN IN PARIS

STATUS REPORT: Location: Côte d'Azur — UPDATE.

Subject Rollo Fusor took two hostages. Haram moved in to rescue; I circled to intercept Fusor's escape.

STEVEN T. SEAGLE & DUNCAN ROULEAU OF **MAN OF ACTION STUDIOS** *Story*

TOM GRUMMETT *Art*

CHRIS SOTOMAYOR *Colors* **COMICRAFT** *Lettering*

On arrival, one hostage dead--dehydrated-- the other--a decoy who attempted to murder Haram.

SKRUSH

I was forced to chose between Fusor's capture and my partner's life.

This should in no way be recorded as another field loss for Haram, though.

If our roles were reversed things would probably have turned out the same... probably.

57

Will Follow new intel and track Fusor in Paris.

IRONIC, HUH? FUSOR WAS MY *FIRST* CASE -- ELEVEN YEARS AGO -- AND I BOTCHED IT --

NOW HE'S MY *LAST* CASE AND I BOTCHED IT AGAIN.

I HAVE *NIGHTMARES* ABOUT HIM, YOU KNOW?

I FOUGHT IN THE GULF -- I'VE SEEN SOME STUFF. BUT SUCKING THE *WATER* OUT OF PEOPLE...?

I WANNA *GET* THIS CREEP SO I CAN *SLEEP* AGAIN.

CLAUDE, WHEN I RETIRE AFTER THIS --

YOU CAN BET THAT'S MY NUMBER ONE PRIORITY -- LONG, PERFECT, SLEEP.

YOU'RE NOT RETIRING, HARAM. YOU DIDN'T BOTCH ANYTHING. THESE TWO ARE *PROS* --

MOVING IN ON LONELY, WEALTHY MEN WITH PROMISES OF MÉNAGE A TROIS AND LORD KNOWS WHAT ELSE --

AND ONCE THEY SUCK THE *RESOURCES* DRY -- FUSOR SUCKS THE "HOST" DRY AND THEY MOVE ON.

THERE'S NO TELLING HOW LONG FUSOR'S ACCOMPLICE WAS IN THERE FIRST. *NEITHER* ONE OF US SPOTTED HER --

I JUST SPOTTED HER.

SSKKTCH

AAAAAH!

WHAT THE --?

THIS SITUATION IS OUT OF CONTROL. *YOU'RE* OUT OF CONTROL. WE NEED TO *WITHDRAW* BEFORE EVERY COP IN PARIS IS ON US --

SHE'S *RABBITING!* WE DON'T KNOW *WHO* SHE IS. WE LET HER GET AWAY NOW, WE'VE...

...LOST HER FOR GOOD...

SKRTCH

SHE'S STILL HERE...

CREEEEEAK

MOVE --!

I'M PINNED! COME LIFT THE -- !

HANG ON! SHE'S *CLOSE.* I CAN STILL *GET* HER --

HARAM!

FOUL LITTLE MAN. YOU MADE ME *RUN...*

I *HATE* RUNNING.

...IT MAKES ME *THIRSTY.*

HNGHH

67

YOU'RE KILLING HIM!

YES, FINALLY.

Y-Y-YOU -- IT W-WAS YOU ALL ALONG -- NNH-NOT FUSOR --!

ROLLO WAS MY CUTE DISTRACTION. HE KEPT YOU OFF MY SCENT FOR YEARS.

BUT, YOU WOULDN'T LEAVE WELL ENOUGH *ALONE*. YOU MADE ROLLO NERVOUS.

...WHICH MADE HIM A LOT LESS CUTE. NOW BE QUIET AND DIE.

SKRTCH

I HEARD THAT. BUT DON'T BOTHER STRUGGLING. YOU'RE --

NEXT --?

YOU'RE NOT THE ONLY ONE WHO'S *SPECIAL* HERE, WITCH!

SKAK

UNFHH!

NNNNN...

HARAM! GET ME OUT! I CAN --

I GOT THIS.

GIVE YA A HAND?

WE WERE SUPPOSED TO BRING HER *IN*.

WE STILL CAN... GO FIND ME A DUST PAN AND A GARBAGE SACK.

THEY WANTED HER *ALIVE!*

AN' SHE WANTED *US DEAD*. LOOK AT ME!

THE COMPANY ISN'T GOING TO BE HAPPY.

HOW AM I SUPPOSED TO COVER FOR YOU? *AGAIN?*

DON'T. TELL 'EM I ENDED THIS ON *MY* TERMS. WHAT'RE THEY GONNA DO? *FIRE* ME? I QUIT.

YOU *CAN'T* QUIT, HARAM. I...I CAN *FIX* ALL THIS IN THE REPORT. FUDGE THE FACTS A LITTLE.

THE ONLY TWO PEOPLE WHO KNOW WHAT HAPPENED HERE ARE *US*.

....WHY WOULD YOU DO THAT FOR ME?

GIVE ME TIME TO FIND A PARTNER I CAN STAND. IT'S HARD ENOUGH OUT HERE WITH SOMEONE YOU CAN *TRUST*.

DO THAT FOR ME. SIX MONTHS, *THEN* RETIRE. WHAT DO YOU SAY?

OKAY, HALF A YEAR. YOU HAVE MY *WORD*.

GOOD. NOW IF YOU COULD DEAL WITH *THEM* -- ?

SON OF A -- WHY DO *I* ALWAYS HAVE TO EXPLAIN EVERYTHING TO THE COPS? I DON'T EVEN SPEAK FRENCH, CLAUDE!

FOR ONCE *I'D* LIKE TO GO INVISIBLE AND MAKE A CLEAN BREAK WITH NO ONE KNOWING I WAS EVER THERE.

End of report.
Delivery Mode: Walk in.
Field Agent Signature:
Claude R

PRIMATECH

YOU'RE ALWAYS SO PUNCTUAL!

MORE THAN I CAN SAY FOR MY PARTNER! IS HE HERE YET?

HE CERTAINLY IS! YOU REMEMBER NOAH BENNET?

I'M LOOKING FORWARD TO WORKING WITH YOU.

NO, I'M YOUR TRAINER. HARAM'S MY PARTNER.

WHERE'S HARAM?

HE'S RETIRED.

NO, HE'S STAYING ON. HALF A YEAR. WE SHOOK -- HE -- GET HIM ON THE PHONE. I WANT TO TALK TO HIM --

I'M AFRAID THAT WON'T BE *POSSIBLE*, CLAUDE. *HE'S RETIRED.*

NOW HURRY IN. MR. THOMPSON IS WAITING FOR YOU BOTH....

End

HEROISM is FOUND in the HEART

CHRISTOPHER ZATTA
Story

RYAN ODAGAWA
Art

JOHN STARR
Colors

COMICRAFT
Lettering

I AM BACK IN TOKYO. WORKING AT YAMAGATO. HIRO LEFT ME HERE SO HE COULD BE A HERO. BECAUSE HE'S THE ONE WITH SUPER POWERS.*

*EDITOR'S NOTE: TRANSLATED FROM JAPANESE.

I'M SPECIAL TOO. I'VE BEEN ON INCREDIBLE ADVENTURES IN AMERICA. I CAN BE A HERO. AND LIKE CLARK KENT AND PETER PARKER, MY DAY JOB IS MY PUBLIC PERSONA.

YOUR POSITION HAS BEEN FILLED. FOR THE TIME BEING, I WILL ASSIGN YOU TO HIRO'S OLD JOB.

KAITO NAKAMURA. CEO. IMPOSING. INTIMIDATING. HIRO'S DAD.

I AM GRATEFUL. BUT WHAT HAPPENS WHEN HIRO RETURNS? WHERE WILL I WORK THEN?

THERE IS NO NEED TO CROSS A BRIDGE, BEFORE YOU HAVE NEED TO CROSS IT, ANDO.

BRIDGE? WHAT DOES THAT MEAN?

KIMIKO!

KIMIKO. BEAUTIFUL. FORMIDABLE. BOSS' DAUGHTER. EXECUTIVE VICE PRESIDENT. AND THE GATE-KEEPER OF MY LONELY HEART.

HEY, KIMIKO. IT'S ME... *ANDO*... HIRO'S FRIEND?

OH, RIGHT. HELLO.

SHE'S PLAYING IT COOL. AS IF SHE DIDN'T REMEMBER ME. I KNOW THAT GAME. I'LL SHOW HER COOL. LIKE A TRUE SUPERHERO.

SO, THAT BROTHER OF YOURS. LET ME TELL YOU, THIS ONE TIME IN A VEGAS CASINO --

=GROAN= I NEED TO DO SOME WORK. YOU SHOULD BE AT YOUR DESK AS WELL.

SLAM

KIMIKO NAKAMURA
EXECUTIVE VICE PRESIDENT

=SIGH=

EVERY HERO NEEDS A HEROINE.

HERE IT IS. THE *ULTIMATE SHOWDOWN* BEGINS. AM I READY TO FACE THE ENEMY?

GET THE *GIRL* AND *GET RID* OF HER *FRIEND!*

LET'S GET OUT OF HERE!

I CAN USE AGILE AND LIGHTNING QUICK REFLEXES TO ESCAPE. I ONLY HOPE KIMIKO IS OK.

EGAD!

A GREAT WARRIOR KNOWS WHEN IT'S TIME TO RETREAT AND FACE THE ENEMY ANOTHER DAY.

EAT HEEL!

THANKS FOR DIVERTING HIM!

UH, SURE THING... YOU KNOW HOW TO RIDE A MOTORCYCLE?

I'M ON A JOURNEY.

KRAKKOOM

BLACKOUT

TO FIND PEOPLE WITH REMARKABLE ABILITIES.

Part **1** of **2**

MARK SABLE *Story*   **JASON BADOWER** *Art*   **COMICRAFT** *Lettering*

TO *HELP* THEM.

BUT TO HELP THEM I NEED--

MONEY?

AND CREDIBILITY. YOU'RE THE LEADING RESEARCH HOSPITAL IN--

LET ME STOP YOU RIGHT THERE, DR. SURESH.

IT'S A LONELY JOURNEY. WHEREVER I GO, I'M MET WITH DISBELIEF. I CAN'T BLAME THEM. WITHOUT SEEING THE PROOF I HAVE...IT'S NO WONDER THE WORLD IS, WELL...

SHOONK

...IN THE DARK.

LET ME ASK YOU SOMETHING, SURESH. CAN ANY OF THESE *"REMARKABLE"* PEOPLE YOU CLAIM TO HAVE ENCOUNTERED RAISE THE DEAD?

WELL, NOT EXACTLY...

BECAUSE FOR THE PAST THREE WEEKS WE'VE HAD POWER OUTAGES. THAT MEANS DEAD PATIENTS. AND WORSE--*LAWSUITS.*

WHICH MEANS PRETTY SOON WE WON'T HAVE THE MONEY TO KEEP OUR PATIENTS ALIVE, LET ALONE FUND YOUR PSEUDO-SCIENCE.

NOW IF YOU'LL EXCUSE ME, I HAVE A *MEDICAL FACILITY* TO RUN.

IT'S NOT POLITE TO STARE.

I'M DYING. NO ONE KNOWS WHY. I'VE MADE MY PEACE WITH THAT. I DON'T NEED YET ANOTHER DOCTOR POKING AROUND MY CHARTS, THINKING THIS TIME HE HAS THE MIRACLE CURE.

UNLESS...YOU'RE HERE TO BRING ME THAT BOOK. A LITTLE READING'S ALL I'VE GOT THESE DAYS. HOSPITAL LIBRARY'S NOT WHAT I'D CALL *EXTENSIVE*, THOUGH.

SHANTI...

EXCUSE ME?

MY SISTER. SHE HAD THE SAME SYMPTOMS YOU DO.

MEANING...

YOU'RE NOT ALONE. AND I CAN HELP YOU.

WHAT ARE YOU DOING?

GETTING READY TO *CURE* YOU. GIVING YOU MY *BLOOD*.

YOUR BLOOD. IS THAT WHAT CURED YOUR SISTER?

NO...SHE DIED BEFORE I WAS BORN. BUT I WAS ABLE TO SAVE SOMEONE ELSE, SOMEONE SPECIAL.

LIKE THE PEOPLE YOU WERE TELLING THE DIRECTOR ABOUT. ARE YOU ONE OF THEM?

I'M AFRAID NOT.

90

I GREW UP THINKING I WAS AN ONLY CHILD. FOR ALL INTENTS AND PURPOSES, I *WAS* ALONE.

RECENTLY I LEARNED THAT I HAD A SISTER. SHE HAD REMARKABLE ABILITIES. BUT ALONG WITH THOSE ABILITIES CAME THE DISEASE WHICH CLAIMED HER LIFE.

YESTERDAY I THOUGHT I FOUND SOMEONE ELSE WITH THE *SAME* DISEASE. SOMEONE I COULD HELP. SOMEONE I COULD *SAVE*.

BLACKOUT

SZZZZZZKKZZT

I WAS WRONG ON ALL COUNTS.

Part 2 of 2

MARK SABLE *Story*   **JASON BADOWER** *Art*   **COMICRAFT** *Lettering*

OH MY GOD. IT'S *YOU.*

94

SHOONK

SZZZIIIZZZZT

ARGHHHHHHH!

DID I...

NO...HE'LL LIVE. BUT HE, AND THE PEOPLE HE WORKS FOR, THEY'LL KEEP COMING FOR YOU. WHICH IS WHY I HAVE TO GET YOU TO--

SCREEEEEECH

THUD

WHAT ARE YOU DOING?

WHEREVER I GO, I'LL CAUSE TRAFFIC ACCIDENTS. ZAP PEOPLE'S PACEMAKERS. MAYBE BRING A PLANE DOWN.

I WAS AT PEACE WITH DYING... BUT I'LL NEVER BE AT PEACE WITH KILLING AGAIN. THIS IS THE ONLY WAY!

NO, IT'S NOT. FOLLOW THE MAP INSIDE THE PACK. THERE SHOULD BE ENOUGH PROVISIONS TO TAKE YOU SOMEPLACE... SOMEPLACE WHERE YOU CAN'T HURT ANYBODY.

I PROMISE I'LL COME BACK AND HELP YOU. YOU'LL HEAL. AND MAYBE, IN TIME... WE'LL FIND A WAY FOR YOU TO USE YOUR ABILITY TO HELP PEOPLE, NOT HURT THEM.

ONE MORE THING. I WANT YOU TO HAVE THIS.

WHEN I WAS GROWING UP...MY FATHER WAS...WELL, HE WAS VERY DEDICATED TO HIS WORK. BUT WHILE HE WAS AWAY, I WOULD READ HIS BOOKS. EVEN IF I DIDN'T UNDERSTAND THEM...

...I NEVER FELT ALONE.

ACTIVATING EVOLUTION

Fin

〈"...GO BACK TO THE SCENE AND FIND OUT 'WHO'?"〉

〈THE BOY KNOWS WHO!〉

〈"THESE PEOPLE WHERE POISONED BY SOMEBODY."〉

〈TELL HIM WHAT YOU SAW!〉

Let's take human flight as an example.

〈IT'S NOT THE BLACK PLAGUE LIKE THEY ARE SAYING ON TV! HE SAW SOMEONE DO THIS!〉

One can imagine the ability to fly would enhance a person's chance of survival AND be attractive to the opposite sex. This makes choice easy.

〈HE SAW THE DEVIL!〉

But, as a contrast, there are mutations that could harm the positive evolution of a species.

Like the ability to host a deadly virus.

〈WANT TO HELP ME?〉

Naturally, this type of trait is often rejected because...

...if left unchecked, the worst cases of scenarios can occur...

⟨WANT TO HELP ME CAPTURE THE DEVIL?⟩

...the extinction of the species.

MAYA y ALEJANDRO

MARK WARSHAW *Story*
RYAN ODAGAWA *Art*
JOHN STARR *Colors*
COMICRAFT *Lettering*

But in some cases...

⟨YOU SAW HER HERE?⟩

...the very mutation that seems most destructive...

⟨THERE WERE TWO?⟩

...can be cured, corrected or eradicated.

⟨SO IT WAS A BOY AND A GIRL?⟩

Or, better yet...

⟨WANT TO HELP ME DRAW A PICTURE?⟩

...take the virtually immortal cancer cell. Some scientists believe it actually holds the secret to keeping healthy cells alive longer.

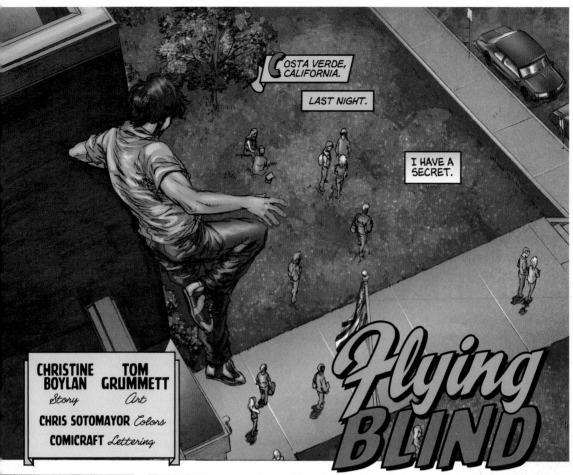

COSTA VERDE, CALIFORNIA.

LAST NIGHT.

I HAVE A SECRET.

CHRISTINE BOYLAN *Story*

TOM GRUMMETT *Art*

CHRIS SOTOMAYOR *Colors*

COMICRAFT *Lettering*

Flying **BLIND**

I LIKE TO FLY WITH MY EYES CLOSED.

OH, DON'T WORRY. I'M PERFECTLY SAFE UP HERE.

YOU'D BE SURPRISED. PEOPLE EXIST MOSTLY AT EYE LEVEL.

TAKES A CERTAIN KIND OF PERSON TO LOOK...*UP.*

YOU CAN FLY BLIND WITHOUT RADAR OR SOME SIXTH SENSE.

WE LIVE IN THE TROPOSPHERE, FOR EXAMPLE. ONE LAYER IN A MANY-LAYERED ATMOSPHERE, AND WITHIN THE TROPOSPHERE ARE EVEN MORE LAYERS.

TO ME, EACH OF THOSE LAYERS HAS A DIFFERENT SCENT. ONE OF THEM, AND I MEAN THIS SINCERELY, SMELLS LIKE PIZZA.

AND THE TROPOSPHERE?

IT'S FULL OF WATER VAPOR.

SO MUCH MORE FUN THAN RUNNING THROUGH A SPRINKLER.

I'M NOT SHOWING OFF. THERE'S NO ONE AROUND TO SHOW OFF TO, RIGHT?

BUT I LOVE HITTING THE STRATOSPHERE.

THOUGH IT'S BEST TO BRING A SWEATER.

THE PLANES ARE NO TROUBLE ONCE YOU LEARN TO STAY OUT OF THE AIRWAYS...

...AND IF YOU KNOW ALL THE EXIT RAMPS, IT'S WAY EASIER TO NAVIGATE THAN THE 405 FREEWAY.

THE AIR GETS THIS AMAZING SMELL AS YOU ALMOST COME BACK DOWN TO EARTH. THE WARMTH OF ROOTS AND PLANTS AND TREES, THE HEAT OF PEOPLE.

AND WHAT'D I TELL YOU?

NO ONE LOOKS UP.

ROBOTS *CAN'T* LOOK UP.

COSTA VERDE, CALIFORNIA.

THIS MORNING.

SEE, I HAVE THIS THEORY.

WHETHER IT'S FATE OR CHOICE...

...PEOPLE BREAK DOWN INTO ONLY TWO CATEGORIES.

YOU'RE EITHER A *ROBOT* OR AN *ALIEN*.

MY DEBATE TEACHER WOULD CALL THAT REDUCTIVE.

I CALL IT A NEAT EXPRESSION OF A LARGER TRUTH.

ROBOTS OPERATE OUT OF PROGRAMS...

...*CONVENTIONAL* LOGIC.

THEY FOLLOW THE RULES.

ROBOTS SCAN THE WORLD FROM SIDE TO SIDE.

ALIENS ARE MORE... ABSTRACT THINKERS.

IF THEY NEED TO BREAK A RULE TO KEEP TO THEIR OWN PATHS, THEY DO. WITHOUT FEAR.

ALIENS LOOK DOWN AND UP...WHEN THEY CHOOSE TO.

I'M NOT CONDEMNING ONE OR THE OTHER, BUT...

...I'D RATHER BE ALONE THAN BE SURROUNDED BY ROBOTS.

AND ROBOTS COULD NEVER EVEN SEE SOMEONE LIKE ME.

PORT-AU-PRINCE, HAITI

"...THEN THE CONTACT WILL GET YOU TO COSTA VERDE, CALIFORNIA. *BENNET* SAYS YOU KNOW HOW TO FIND HIM FROM THERE."

MEANWHILE, *THE COMPANY* WILL FIND ME HERE, "STUNNED AND BEWILDERED." DISAPPOINTED, SURELY, BUT NONE THE WISER...

I'M SORRY... DON'T YOU NEED TO WRITE ANY OF THIS DOWN?

MEMORY IS NOT AN ISSUE FOR ME.

DO NOT WORRY, *DR. SURESH.* THE PLAN IS SOUND. I WILL GET TO BENNET...

...IF GOD TRULY BELIEVES I DESERVE TO.

I DON'T KNOW ABOUT GOD, BUT MY *FATHER* USED TO SAY THAT ALL MEN DESERVED A SECOND CHANCE...GOOD MEN DESERVED THREE.

WHATEVER YOU DID WITH THE COMPANY... THIS IS YOUR OPPORTUNITY TO MAKE IT RIGHT, BY HELPING US TAKE THEM *DOWN.*

CONSIDER YOURSELF BLESSED TO HAVE HAD...SUCH A *COMPASSIONATE* FATHER.

I WILL JOIN YOUR CRUSADE, SURESH... BUT FIRST...

"...THERE IS SOMETHING I MUST DO."

THE CROSSROADS. I HAVE NOT BEEN HERE SINCE THE DAY MY FATHER THREW HIMSELF FROM ITS PEAK...

NOTHING HAS CHANGED. EVERYTHING HAS CHANGED.

The CROSSROADS

JOE KELLY OF **MAN OF ACTION STUDIOS**
Story

MICHAEL GAYDOS
Art

CHRIS SOTOMAYOR *Colors*   **COMICRAFT** *Lettering*

I DO NOT PRACTICE THE *OLD WAYS* AS MY FATHER DID...

...BUT ONE CANNOT BE THE CHILD OF A GREAT *HOUNGAN* AND FAIL TO LEARN HOW TO MAKE CONTACT WITH *LES INVISIBLES*. *SPIRITS*.

I KNOW MY *HERBS*. I KNOW MY *SYMBOLS*.

THE SUMMONING CEREMONY IS A SIMPLE MATTER REALLY, ESPECIALLY HERE, WHERE THE VEIL BETWEEN LIGHT AND SHADE IS AT ITS THINNEST...

...SIMPLE AS DYING.

I KNEW *THEY* WOULD APPEAR TO ME FIRST...BUT I DID NOT ANTICIPATE HOW MUCH IT WOULD *HURT.*

THE PEOPLE OF MY VILLAGE. FRIENDS, *FAMILY,* WHOSE MINDS I SCRAPED CLEAN AS A YOUNG BOY, UNTRAINED IN MY "*GIFT*" AND TERRIFIED FOR MY FATHER'S LIFE.

OF ALL THAT I HAVE DONE, *THEY* REPRESENT MY GREATEST SINS...AT LEAST, THAT IS WHAT I BELIEVE...

UNTIL THEY BEGIN TO *WHISPER.*

THEY TELL THE TALES OF MY TRANSGRESSIONS. NOT JUST AGAINST THEM...

...BUT AGAINST EVERY PERSON I'VE EVER "*BAGGED AND TAGGED*" IN THE NAME OF "*THE COMPANY.*" *EVERY ONE.*

IT TAKES HALF THE NIGHT.

I WANT TO BEG FOR *FORGIVENESS,* BUT I MUST NOT.

PENITENCE IS *WEAKNESS* ACCORDING TO THE *OLD WAYS.* TO SURVIVE, I MUST *ACCEPT* WHAT THE SPIRITS GIVE ME AND *ENDURE* WHO I HAVE BEEN...

...IF I AM EVER TO *BECOME* SOMETHING ELSE.

111

SOMETHING ELSE?!

AS GROWS THE VINE SO GROWS THE FRUIT! YOU ARE YOUR FATHER'S SON! HE WHO WAS FAVORED BY THE LOA WITH POWER BUT SOUGHT ONLY SELFISH GAINS!

YOU ARE WEAK! YOU ARE BROKEN! YOU WILL DIE HERE AS HE DID BEFORE YOU!

WHY DID YOU COME HERE?! FORGIVENESS?!

I CAME FOR A BLESSING. FROM YOU. FROM THE LOA. FROM THOSE WRETCHED WHO HAVE FALLEN BECAUSE OF MY ARROGANCE AND BLINDNESS...

BECAUSE I WANT MY LIFE TO COUNT FOR SOMETHING GOOD BEFORE IT IS TOO LATE.

I CAME HERE, BECAUSE...

I THOUGHT WE DIDN'T WANT TO KNOW?

WE, HUH?

I WANNA TAKE YOU ON A DATE, CAITLIN.

A PROPER DATE.

THIS THE TIME TO BE TALKING OF DATES?

WHAT WITH ALL THIS GLOWERING AND LOOMING AND NARY A SPARK OF LIGHTNING?

"HOW ABOUT A WALK ON THE BEACH, THEN? PROPER ENOUGH?"

"YEAH. YOU CAN TELL ME A STORY."

PETRIFIED LIGHTNING

CHRISTINE BOYLAN *Story*

MICHAEL GAYDOS *Art*

EDGAR AT STUDIO F *Colors*

COMICRAFT *Lettering*

"WHILE HE WAITED FOR HIS WEAPONS TO BE MADE, HE WALKED ALONG THE STRAND NEAR THE SMITHY, IMPATIENT TO GET OUT AND GET CONQUERING."

"ONE DAY HE SAW SOMETHING GLISTEN IN THE SAND. SOMETHING THAT CAME FROM SO DEEP WITHIN NATURE THAT IT SEEMED... *UN*NATURAL."

"WHAT HE SAW WAS TEEVAL, YOUNG QUEEN OF THE SEVEN SEAS. A *MERMAID*."

MERMAID?!

EXCUSE ME? YOU OF ALL PEOPLE OUGHT TO BELIEVE IN WILD CREATURES.

ARE YOU CALLING ME A WILD --

OW! *DAMMIT!*

STOP MESSING ABOUT AND PAY ATTENTION, OR NO MORE STORIES.

SORRY.

"SO CÚCHULAINN, THIS GOD, THIS BIG DUMB HERO, COMES LUMBERING PAST AND SEES THE SLEEPING QUEEN OF THE SEA."

"AND THE SIMPLE BRUTE, IRELAND'S GREATEST MAN, TIES HER UP."

"WHAT KIND OF STORY *IS* THIS, CAITLIN?"

"SHHH.

"WELL, SHE WOKE UP IN A RIGHT RAGE AT FIRST -- FORGETTING HER OWN POWER AT THE SHOCK OF HER PREDICAMENT.

WHAP

"BUT SHE SOON RECOVERED HERSELF.

"SHE LOOKED HIM DEAD IN THE EYE. SHE KNEW HIM. SHE NAMED HIM."

"AND SHE MADE HIM AN OFFER."

LET ME GO, MORTAL.

NO. I CAN'T. I'LL LOSE YOU.

UNBIND ME, AND I WILL GIVE YOU SOMETHING MORE USEFUL THAN MYSELF.

BUT I...I LOVE YOU.

DON'T BE FOOLISH. DO YOU WANT TO CONQUER THE LAND OR DROWN WITH ME IN THE SEA?

GO TO THE SMITHY. TELL THE ARTISAN TO CARVE MY NAME AND IMAGE ON THE INSIDE OF YOUR SHIELD, JUST AS YOU SEE ME NOW.

IN BATTLE, LOOK YOU ON THE SHIELD AND CALL MY NAME, AND YOUR STRENGTH WILL BE MULTIPLIED EVEN AS YOUR ENEMIES WEAKEN AND FALL.

"AND IT CAME TO PASS. CÚCHULAINN RECEIVED HIS SWORD AND SHIELD, AND CALLED UPON TEEVAL'S STRENGTH IN BATTLE."

"HE CONQUERED ULSTER, BECAME KING, AND IS STILL HERALDED AS IRELAND'S GREATEST HERO. THE BIG DAMN LUG."

SHE GAVE HIM HIS POWER.

IF YOU LIKE. *OR* SHE SHOWED HIM HIS OWN POWER. TRICK OF THE MIND.

BUT HE LOST HER.

HE DID AT THAT.

LET'S SEE IF IT WORKS.

WHAT?

CAITLIN!

YOUR NAME WORKS, CAITLIN!

THIS IS WHAT HAPPENS WHEN LIGHTNING HITS THE BEACH. IT MAKES *GLASS.* THEY'RE CALLED FULGURITES.

PETRIFIED LIGHTNING.

I CAN HEAR WHAT YOU'RE THINKING.

I KNOW. LET'S GO HOME.

The End

ODESSA, RUSSIA, 18 YEARS AGO.

HE WENT THROUGH THERE!

STAY OUT OF THE WAY, NOAH. LET US SHOW YOU HOW *REAL* COMPANY MEN HUNT.

YOU'RE THE BOSS.

MY FIRST *"BAG AND TAG."* THE COMPANY'S NEW PROGRAM TO KEEP TABS ON THE GENETICALLY GIFTED.

THE COMPANY DECIDED TO GO WITH A LESS... *LETHAL* WAY OF DEALING WITH THOSE WITH ABILITIES. TRAP 'EM, TAG 'EM, AND RELEASE 'EM. LIKE... BIOLOGISTS, OUT IN THE FIELD.

I'M HERE ON THIS TRAINING EXERCISE TO TAKE NOTES. SEE HOW UPPER MANAGEMENT IS AT HANDLING THE NEW OPERATING SYSTEM.

I'VE NEVER BEEN MUCH OF AN OBSERVER -- I'M MORE THE *HANDS-ON* TYPE. LET'S SEE IF I CAN'T GET MY HANDS DIRTY A *LITTLE* THOUGH.

TEAM BUILDING EXERCISE

PIERLUIGI COTHRAN
Story

TRAVIS KOTZEBUE
Art

JOHN STARR
Colors

COMICRAFT
Lettering

WE WOULDN'T WANT *THEM* HAVING ALL THE *FUN* NOW, WOULD WE?

SITUATIONS ARE *INVALUABLE* FOR US.

WE LEARN ABOUT THEIR INABILITY TO SEE THEMSELVES AS SOMETHING *MORE* THAN HUMAN. FOR THE MOST PART, THESE ANOMALIES FEAR *THEMSELVES* AS MUCH AS THEY FEAR *US*.

SO WHEN THEY ARE GIVEN THE CHOICE OF FIGHT OR FLIGHT, NINETY-NINE TIMES OUT OF A HUNDRED, WE KNOW THEY CHOOSE *FLIGHT*.

KNOWING THIS, WE CAN SET THE CAGE SO THEY FLY RIGHT *INTO* IT.

QUARANTINE

JIM MARTIN *Story*   **MARCUS TO** *Penciler*   **MARK ROSLAN** *Digital Inks*   **BETH SOTELO** *Colors*   **COMICRAFT** *Lettering*

THE VIRUS WAS SPREADING TOO FAST TO STAY IN THE CITY... THE PARANOIA, THE IRRATIONALITY, THE FEAR...

IT'S TERRIFYING -- A VIRUS REDUCING AN AMERICAN CITY INTO A THIRD WORLD EPIDEMIC.

WE'D BEEN TRYING TO CONTAIN THE VIRUS FOR MOST OF THE MONTH...THIS WAS THE THIRD ATTEMPT WE'D MADE AT QUARANTINING A COMMUNITY --

IT WAS ALSO OUR LAST. TOO MANY PEOPLE WERE ALREADY SICK, DYING OR DEAD... IT'S A MIRACLE WE'RE ALIVE.

I HAD BEEN WORKING OUT OF THE CDC'S PITTSBURGH OFFICES TO HELP WITH THE OVERFLOW... THAT'S WHEN THEY DECLARED A NATIONAL EMERGENCY.

CLIK POP HSSS

DEPARTMENT OF ...AND SECURITY
LEMAY, HOWARD

IT TOOK ME *TWO HOURS* TO GET ATLANTA ON THE LINE. THEY HAD BEEN SLAMMED WITH CALLS SINCE THE OUTBREAKS STARTED -- IT'S *SPREADING...*

HELP!

WHAT THE--?!

PRRIINNNNNGGG

MASKS ON! EVERYONE! REMAIN *CALM* AND PUT YOUR *MASKS* ON!

THE QUARANTINE'S BEEN BREACHED!

HOWARD?! HOWARD!!! SAVE US... HELP!

DON'T LEAVE ME... THE VIRUS, IT'S *IN* HERE...

LET ME OUT -- *PLEASE!*

I... I *CAN'T...* YOU'RE *INFECTED.*

BUT... I MIGHT NOT EVEN *HAVE* IT!

BUT YOU *MIGHT...*

KA-CHUNK

AND *I* DON'T WANT TO *DIE...*

BUT -- I'M YOUR *WIFE!!!*

THE VIRUS IS DESTROYING EVERYTHING IT TOUCHES.

LAYING ITSELF UPON US LIKE A BLANKET OF DEATH.

IF IT TOOK THIS LONG TO SHOW IN DYLAN, *ANYONE* COULD HAVE IT...

EVEN *ME...*

The End

FIRE STATION #5, LAS VEGAS, NEVADA.

CAPTAIN BURKE HAD IT OUT FOR ME FROM DAY ONE OF FIREFIGHTER TRAINING.

TRAINEE CLASS OF 20

HAWKINS -- YOU'RE SAVING *LIVES* WITH THAT WATER, NOT FILLING A DAMN POOL -- MOVE FASTER!

I'M BEATIN' EVERYBODY!

MAN ON FIRE

TIMM KEPPLER
Story

MICHAEL GAYDOS
Art

CHRIS SOTOMAYOR
Colors

COMICRAFT
Lettering

IN THE CLASSROOM. DURING DRILLS. MAN, HE NEVER LET UP.

TWO MONTHS LATER...

I TRIED TO SET THINGS RIGHT.

I GOT A FAMILY *TOO* -- JUST WANNA DO RIGHT BY THEM.

ALL DUE RESPECT SIR, YOU DON'T KNOW A *THING* ABOUT ME.

I KNOW THE KIND OF FAMILY MAN *YOU* ARE.

I KNOW YOU AREN'T GONNA BE A *FIREFIGHTER.*

TEST DAY...

STOP! HAND YOUR PAPERS TO LIEUTENANT PALMER, GET SUITED UP -- TIME FOR THE *REAL* TEST!

IT WAS A MOCK FIRE. THE TEST: SAVE THE DUMMY DOLLS INSIDE, PUT OUT THE FIRE, GET OUT SAFE.

WE WORK IN TEAMS. YOU HAVE TEN MINUTES. SUCCESS AND YOU *PASS* -- ANYTHING LESS AND YOU *FAIL.* GOT THAT? HAWKINS?

I GOT STUCK WITH *BURKE.* LUCKY ME.

LIGHT IT UP!

REMEMBER: VENTILATE! PROTECT EXPOSURE! KEEP AN EYE ON EACH OTHER!

WE SHOULDA NOTICED THE FIRE WAS TOO HOT. TOO BIG. BUT *ADRENALINE* GOT IN THE WAY.

KRAKK

SECURE THE BEDROOM -- MEET IN THE KITCHEN!

COPY THAT!

KAPOWW

HAWKINS!

IT'S *TOO HOT* -- I CAN'T *PASS!*

PALMER -- THE *GAS LINE* -- IT'S SET TOO *HIGH!* THE SHUT-OFF VALVE'S IN THE *BASEMENT!* SOUTHEAST CORNER!

CAN'T GET IN, CAPTAIN -- IT'S *COLLAPSED!*

GET *OUTTA HERE,* HAWKINS!

KRKSSH

I'M NOT *LEAVIN'* YOU!

GOT NO MORE THAN *30 SECONDS* 'FORE EVERYTHING *FALLS!*

HAWKINS! THERE'S NO *TIME!*

I HAD TO SAVE EVERYONE. AND THE FASTEST WAY TO THE BASEMENT WAS *STRAIGHT DOWN.*

I DON'T EVEN *REMEMBER* RUNNIN' THROUGH THE BASEMENT.

I WAS THINKIN' ABOUT *MICAH*.

AND HOW MUCH HE'D LOVE TO SEE ME USING MY *POWERS* LIKE THAT.

HMMPH!

SSFPHH*HM*MM

I TOOK MY TIME TO ROAM THE HAVOC.

ABSORBING THE CLUES THAT WOULD LEAD ME TO MY *NEW TARGET.*

THE MEN DID NOT UNDERSTAND THE MISSION.

NO MAN IS LOYAL AT HEART. I HAVE FOUND THIS COUNTLESS TIMES.

THIS IS BOUND TO BE ANOTHER DARK NIGHT.

AYE, WHO WOULD *SEARCH* FOR THE ARMY CAPABLE OF THIS?

HE WOULD.

FEAR WOULD KEEP THEM IN LINE FAR BETTER.

IT WAS *HIM.* I KNEW IT INSTANTLY.

I HAD BEEN *PURPOSELESS* FOR SO LONG. WANTING NOTHING OTHER THAN TO DESTROY THE *MISERABLE HUMANITY* THAT SURROUNDED ME.

I WAS A GOD. *TIMELESS.* BUT EVEN A MAN'S DYING WHISPER OF *HIS* POWER CHALLENGED MY CLAIM.

SO *ENDING* HIM BECAME MY *NEW PURPOSE.*

149

WHAT BUSINESS HAVE YOU HERE?

I HUNT THE SEPARATISTS WHO LAID WASTE TO ARLESBURGH.

THEN *I* AM YOUR MAN.

YOU *ALONE?* THE SAME MAN SAID TO BE *UNKILLABLE?*

MY NAME IS *EVAN,* AND THESE WALLS THAT ONCE LOOMED ABOVE MY PEOPLE FELL IN UNDER AN *HOUR.*

SURELY *YOUR* SWORD IS NO *THREAT* TO ME.

LEAVE NOW AND YOUR TRESSPASS WILL BE *FORGIVEN.*

HE WAS EITHER *INSANE* OR A FEARSOME OPPONENT.

I HAD TO KNOW *WHICH.*

DO YOU *STILL* CLAIM TO BE THE ONE WHO CANNOT BE *KILLED?*

I *DO!*

THEN *PROVE* IT!

PITY. TOO YOUNG FOR SUCH BIG BLUFFS.

NO!

COMMANDER!

150

THERE WERE *TOO MANY* OF THEM. FIGHT AS WE *COULD*, WE TOOK HEAVY LOSSES.

FALL BACK YOU FOOLS! *RETREAT!*

PUSH *ANY* HUMAN TO A CERTAIN LIMIT, AND NOT EVEN *FEAR* WILL KEEP THEM IN LINE.

ONCE AGAIN, I HAD BEEN *ABANDONED.*

SO I *FOUGHT ON* THE ONLY WAY I KNEW *HOW.*

BY *MYSELF.* KILLING AS MANY AS *POSSIBLE.* QUICKLY. WITHOUT *MERCY.*

TIME *PAUSED* AS THIS MAN FELL FROM MY BLADE FOR THE *SECOND TIME* TONIGHT.

AND SOMETHING TOLD ME I MAY BE GETTING THE *FIGHT* I HAD ASKED FOR.

I HAD KILLED THIS MAN ONCE BEFORE...

LAZARUS RISEN!

AND NOW HE FALLS *AGAIN* BY MY BLADE.

THIS WAS NOT A MAN WHO *RETURNED* FROM DEATH AS *I* DID...

THIS WAS A MAN WHO HAD DIED A THOUSAND TIMES. WHILE HIS *BROTHERS* LIVED.

PUTS THINGS INTO PERSPECTIVE.

WOULDN'T YOU SAY?

SUDDENLY THE *WAR* SEEMS LESS IMPORTANT--

AND ALL THAT'S LEFT IS *YOU* --

AND *ME.*

AND *ME.*

AND *ME.*

PURSUIT *Part Two*

OLIVER GRIGSBY *Story*   TOM GRUMMETT *Art*

EDGAR AT STUDIO F   COMICRAFT

Colors   *Lettering*

WE ARE THE *PEOPLE.*

OUR STRENGTH *UNITED.*

AND *YOU...*

...ARE *ALONE.*

IN DEFEAT THE TRUTH *RAGED* AT ME.

I *WAS* ALONE...

WHILE *GODS* SHOULD HAVE *DISCIPLES.*

The End

NOBODY UNDERSTANDS ME.

HECK, I'M NOT EVEN SURE IF I UNDERSTAND MYSELF.

ODESSA, TX.

I LOOK AROUND, AND EVERYONE SEEMS TO *GET* IT, SEEMS TO KNOW WHERE THEY FIT IN.

ST. LOUIS, MO.

LIKE THEY WERE *BORN* WITH A ROADMAP TO WHO THEY WANT TO *BE*.

THEN WHY DID *I* FEEL SO UN-SPECIAL?

WHAT HAPPENED TO THE *SENTRA*?

MR. MUGGLES HAD AN *ACCIDENT*. THAT'S ALL I'M AT LIBERTY TO SAY.

SO IF YOU HAVE *DAD'S* CAR...

LIKE I WAS JUST GOING THROUGH THE *MOTIONS*.

...WHAT'S *HE* DRIVING?

HE'S ON A DAY TRIP. FOR WORK.

EVERYTHING AROUND HERE WAS *PREDICTABLE.*

I JUST WISH I COULD *GO* SOMEWHERE. *ANYWHERE.* WHERE SOMETHING *EXCITING* WOULD HAPPEN.

CLAIRE! I'M GOING TO PICK UP YOUR DAD! YOU *COMIN'?*

TAKE IT WHERE YOU CAN *GET* IT, I GUESS.

I HAD *NO IDEA* WHAT WAS HAPPENING.

HAS HE *MANIFESTED* YET?

I DON'T *BELIEVE* SO.

GET THE READINGS YOU NEED. Q.C. HIS *TRACKING TAG.* THEN GET HIM CLEARED FOR *CHECK OUT.*

YES, SIR.

AND BE CAREFUL. *GENTLE.* HE'S JUST A *KID.*

OF COURSE.

ALL I KNEW IS THAT I WANTED TO BE *HOME.*

SPECIAL

JOE POKASKI *Story*   MICHAEL GAYDOS *Art*   CHRIS SOTOMAYOR *Colors*   COMICRAFT *Lettering*

CAN I GO IN AND *GET* HIM?

THAT'S A NEW *LAND-SPEED* RECORD FOR THE FULL COMPLEMENT OF TESTS.

WHAT WAS *UP* WITH THAT WHOLE *"BE GENTLE"* SPEECH?

MAYBE THE OLD MAN IS GOING *SOFT.*

NOT *THAT* OLD MAN.

I NEEDED TO GET OUT OF HERE. *NOW.*

THERE'S SOMETHING *ABOUT* DAD'S PAPER FACTORY.

MATECH PAPER CO.

ODESSA, TEXAS

SOMETHING'S *HAPPENING....*

I LIKED TO PRETEND THERE WERE *MYSTERIES* BEHIND HERE.

SOMETHING KIND OF *INSANE.*

WHAT THE HECK DID THEY *DO* TO ME?!

AND COULD I USE IT TO GET *OUT* OF HERE?

WHAT KIND OF MYSTERIES WOULD I FIND *TODAY?*

UP THERE. AN *EXIT.*

AT LEAST, I *HOPE.*

HOW AM I *DOING* THIS?

HEY! ARE YOU *ONE* OF THEM?

ONE OF *WHO?*

LISTEN. YOU GOTTA *HELP* ME!

HELP YOU *HOW?* WHAT ARE YOU *DOING* IN THERE?

I DON'T KNOW. WHAT'S YOUR *NAME?*

CLAIRE.

WHAT THE HECK IS GOING *ON?*

CLAIRE. I'VE NEVER SEEN ANYTHING *LIKE* HER BEFORE IN MY LIFE...

LISTEN. I NORMALLY AM KIND OF *INTIMIDATED* BY SUPER-PRETTY GIRLS LIKE YOU, BUT YOU GOTTA *HELP* ME.

DID HE JUST CALL ME *PRETTY?*

HOW DID YOU GET *IN* THERE?

HERE'S THE *THING,* I DON'T REALLY *KNOW,* BUT...

LOOK OUT! *BEHIND* YOU!

CLAIRE!

THANK GOD, IT'S DAD. *HE'LL* KNOW WHAT TO DO.

DAD, THERE'S A *BOY,* IN THE VENTS. HE'S IN *TROUBLE.*

WHAT?

I'M TELLING THE *TRUTH.* I *SWEAR.*

I *BELIEVE* YOU. LET ME CHECK.

HELLO?

SWEETIE, THERE'S *NO ONE* THERE.

DID I JUST *IMAGINE* ALL OF THAT?

WHY DOES IT SUDDENLY ALL FEEL LIKE A *DREAM?*

SO MUCH FOR *ADVENTURE*. MAYBE AN ORDINARY DAY ISN'T THAT BAD.

I HAVE NO IDEA WHERE I *WAS* ALL OF YESTERDAY.

ALL I REMEMBER IS THAT *MAN*.

THOSE *HORN RIMMED GLASSES*.

MAYBE EVERYONE ELSE IS *SCARED* LIKE ME. LIKE THAT *BOY*, REAL OR IMAGINED.

MAYBE IT'S JUST PART OF THE *JOB*.

MAYBE I *AM* PRETTY. OR MAYBE I CAN *BE*...

WHATEVER HAPPENED, JUNIOR HIGH DOESN'T FEEL THAT *SCARY* TO ME ANYMORE.

MAYBE THAT LITTLE BIT OF ADVENTURE CAN *INSPIRE* ME A BIT.

MAKE ME MORE ADVENTUROUS.

MAYBE I'LL TRY OUT FOR *CHEERLEADING*.

WHO KNOWS...

MAYBE I *AM* SPECIAL.

The End

166

I THOUGHT I MADE MYSELF PERFECTLY CLEAR *LAST* TIME, ELLE. I *DON'T* WANT YOU HANGING AROUND MY DAUGHTER ANYMORE.

SORRY, MR. BENNET. I'M JUST FOLLOWING *ORDERS* -- KEEP AN EYE ON CLAIRE.

THAT'S *MY* JOB.

YEAH. YOU JUST KEEP *BELIEVING* THAT.

BUT DON'T WORRY --

ONCE CLAIRE MANIFESTS HER BIG BAD *POWER*, *I'LL* BE HER TRAINER.

I JUST MADE UP THAT *LAST* BIT. WISH I COULD SEE HIS FACE. BUT IF I LOOKED, IT'D RUIN THE *COOL* OF IT.

AND I'LL BE JUST AS NICE AS *EDEN* WAS TO ME.

SO, LITTLE MISS POPULAR CHIT CHATTING WITH THE SCHOOL *PARIAH?*

THERE'S A *STORY* THERE.

173

AND QUEENS. WISE MEN
EADERS. PROPHETS AND
ORS. I'VE OUTLIVED THE
TEST MEN AND WOMEN
ON THE PLANET.

EVEN AMONG THOSE WHO
COULD BEND STEEL WITH
THEIR BARE HANDS. OR
WIELD THE VERY ELEMENTS.
I SURVIVED THEM ALL.

ALL EXCEPT
ONE.

*HIRO
NAKAMURA.*

THIS IS
TWICE NOW
THAT HE'S
KILLED ME.

I'VE BEEN ON THIS EARTH
FOR OVER FOUR CENTURIES.

BUT WHAT DO I HAVE
TO *SHOW* FOR IT?

A FEW DOZEN *NAMES?*
TAKEZO KENSEI?
RICHARD SANDERS?
ADAM MONROE?

WHAT GOOD IS *IMMORTALIT*
WHEN YOU'RE *BURIED ALIVE*

WHEN THE

1692, DIEDENSHAUSEN, GERMANY.

AFTER TURNING 42, I REALIZED I DID NOT *AGE*. AFTER 20 YEARS AS MY WIFE, HELENE SAW IT TOO.

SHE FLED INTO THE WOODS, CALLING ME A *DEVIL*. RUMOR HAS IT SHE DIED YEARS LATER IN A NUNNERY.

1747, MILAN, ITALY.

MY SECOND WIFE, MARIA, BORE ME TWO SONS.

EVEN AFTER A CENTURY OF LIVING, I LEARNED SOMETHING *NEW* -- I DON'T LIKE CHILDREN.

I LEFT THEM WITH TWO SACKS OF COIN AND LEFT FOR THE NEW COUNTRY TO BEGIN AGAIN.

1782, I ABANDONED THE QUEEN'S FORCES FOR PARIS, FRANCE.

MY NEXT WIFE I MET AT A BALL AT THE VERSAILLES.

PROUD OF HER LOOKS, I NEVER SAW FREDERICA OUT OF HER FACE POWDER AND ROUGE.

IT WAS THAT LOVE OF LEAD-BASED COSMETICS THAT LED TO HER UNTIMELY END.

1784, JAPAN.

SEARCHING FOR DIRECTION, I RETURNED TO JAPAN TO FIND YAEKO'S DESCENDANTS.

I THOUGHT I COULD FIND FULFILLMENT BY WINNING HER HEART. *OR* HER GREAT-GRANDDAUGHTER'S.

YUMI, WHILE BEAUTIFUL, WAS *NOT* YAEKO. I GREW BORED AND FAKED MY DROWNING WITH A CAREFULLY PLANNED ACCIDENT.

1787- THE NORTHWEST TERRITORY.

I TOOK A NEW NAME AND A NEW WIFE. OUT OF LOVE, I CONFESSED MY SECRET TO HER, THAT I CANNOT DIE.

ANGELICA AND I WERE TOGETHER FOR 62 YEARS, TELLING PEOPLE I WAS HER HUSBAND. THEN SON. THEN GRANDSON.

WE HELD HANDS AS SHE BREATHED HER LAST BREATH, AT AGE 87.

1864 – I MARRIED MY SECOND MARIA IN ATLANTA, AT THE ONSET OF THE CIVIL WAR. AS FATE WOULD HAVE IT, I CHOSE THE LOSING SIDE. *AGAIN.*

WHILE I FOUGHT ON THE BATTLEFIELD, SHE DIED IN A PLANTATION FIRE AFTER INHALING TOO MUCH SMOKE.

MONTREAL 1901 – I PUT MY FRENCH BACK TO GOOD USE AND MET A CAPTIVATING BEAUTY: DIANE.

AFTER A HARSH WINTER, SHE WAS STRICKEN WITH TUBERCULOSIS. AS A LAST MEASURE, I INJECTED HER WITH A VIAL OF MY *BLOOD* AS SHE SLEPT.

THE DOCTORS CALLED HER RECOVERY A *MIRACLE*. SHE DIED A HAPPY AND PEACEFUL DEATH, 20 YEARS LATER.

1926, CHICAGO – LOUISA SAW ME REGENERATE MY LEFT EYE AND SPLEEN AFTER A VICIOUS MUGGING.

EVER THE FRAGILE CREATURE, SHE *DRANK* HERSELF TO DEATH FOUR MONTHS LATER.

1958 – LOS ANGELES.

THERESA NEVER LOVED ME. I LEARNED THIS WHEN SHE AND HER LOVER SHOT ME TWICE IN THE CHEST. THEN DUMPED MY BODY OFF A CLIFF.

BY MORNING, I SWAM BACK TO SHORE AND KILLED THEM AS THEY SLEPT.

1977 – TRINA.

SHE REMARRIED. HAD CHILDREN. GRANDCHILDREN.

DIED SIX YEARS AGO IN A CAR ACCIDENT.

THANKS TO KAITO AND THE OTHERS, I NEVER GOT THE CHANCE TO SAY GOOD-BYE.

AND NOW I AM *ALONE*. DIED MORE TIMES THAN I CAN *COUNT* ALREADY IN THIS COFFIN.

HOW LONG HAS IT BEEN? HOURS? DAYS? WEEKS?

WHAT A *CRUEL* MAN YOU ARE, HIRO NAKAMURA.

BUT THAT SUITS ME *FINE.*

BECAUSE I HAVE MY NEWEST *BRIDE* OUT THERE...

...AND I'M CERTAIN SHE'LL *FIND* ME.

End

...Y EARS AGO...

NAME'S **HAMPTON CONNOLLY.** SOME CALL ME "HAMP," BUT MOST CALL ME "GOOSE."

I WAS DRUCKER'S **PERSONAL PILOT.** I FLEW HIS COMPANY PLANES OVER THE MOUNTAINS **MANY** TIMES BEFORE...

...THIS WOULD BE MY **LAST.**

YOU **SURE** ABOUT THIS?

I GOT IT.

IT'S **BEAUTIFUL.**

GLAD YOU THINK SO. 'CAUSE WE'RE ABOUT TO **CRASH** THERE!

PRESENT DAY...

DRUCKER DECIDED IT WAS *FATE* CALLING HIM HERE. WHO WAS I TO DISAGREE?

PLUS, THE GIRLS WERE NICE AND I DIDN'T HAVE TO BE ANYWHERE. SO WE STAYED. FOR *FIFTEEN YEARS.*

I THOUGHT YOU HAD A *NO-COMPUTER* RULE HERE.

WHAT'S A RULE UNLESS YOU CAN *BREAK* IT.

CLIK

YOU'RE NOT *DRUCKER.*

AND I TAKE IT YOU'RE NOT MY *MASSEUSE.*

NO, I'M CERTAINLY *NOT.* WHERE IS HE?

I DON'T KNOW *WHERE* HE IS.

I HAVEN'T SEEN HIM SINCE THE *CRASH.*

"I SHOULD HAVE NEVER LET HIM *FLY* UNDER SUCH ROUGH CONDITIONS, HE WAS ONLY AN *AMATEUR.*

"THE LOCAL MONKS *TOOK CARE* OF HIM.

"WHEN I WENT TO CHECK ON HIM, HE WAS *GONE...*"

WHERE

IS

HE?

ARRRGGH!

ALL MY LIFE, I'VE HAD TROUBLE MAKING FRIENDS.

IT'S NOT THAT I HAVEN'T *WANTED* FRIENDS...

THEY JUST SEEM TO BE MORE INTERESTED IN WHAT I CAN *DO* THAN WHO I *AM*.

PSST. HEY EINSTEIN, WHAT'S THE AXIS OF SYMMETRY FOR #7?

C'MON, NEUENBERG, WHAT'S THE VALUE OF *X*?

2.38, MEATHEAD.

MATT NEUENBERG!

WHO WON THE WORLD SERIES IN *1968?*

THE DETROIT TIGERS DEFEATED THE ST. LOUIS CARDINALS IN SEVEN GAMES.

WHAT IS THE NUMERICAL VALUE OF *PI?*

3.1415926535...

...8979323846264633...

HOW THE HELL DOES HE KNOW THAT?

THIS HAS GOTTA BE STAGED.

FREAK!!

WEIRDO!!!

BRAINIAC!!!

YOU KNOW, THERE'S A PLACE WHERE BEING *DIFFERENT* IS SEEN AS A *GOOD* THING.

WHO'S *THERE?* WHO *SAID* THAT?

I'M *ELLE.*

I'M HERE TO TAKE YOU SOMEWHERE WHERE YOU'LL FINALLY *FIT IN.*

SUCH A PLACE DOESN'T *EXIST.*

I KNOW WHAT IT'S LIKE TO BE *ALONE.* I PROMISE YOU THIS IS LIKE NOWHERE YOU'VE *BEEN* BEFORE.

AND WHY SHOULD I *BELIEVE* YOU?

OR DO I HAVE A *CHOICE?*

TRUST ME. I'LL *PROTECT* YOU.

WELL, WHAT IF SOMETHING *HAPPENS* TO ME?

WHAT COULD POSSIBLY GO *WRONG?*

HELIX
COMICS

9TH WONDERS!

69
APR

30¢

I'LL ADMIT, I WAS STARTING TO *LIKE* MY NEW HOME. IT KEPT ME BUSY, AND KEPT MY BRAIN CONSTANTLY STIMULATED.

BUT I NEVER LET ON HOW *MUCH* I LIKED IT. OR HOW MUCH I LIKED *HER.*

SAVING THE WORLD, ONE *VIRUS* AT A TIME?

MORE LIKE SAVING THE WORLD, ONE *DULL LINE OF CODE* AT A TIME. I DIDN'T KNOW THIS WOULD BE SO *REPETITIVE.*

WHAT YOU'RE DOING IS *IMPORTANT,* MATT. DON'T CUT YOURSELF SHORT. BESIDES, IT'S BETTER THAN A *DORM ROOM,* RIGHT?

YOU MEAN MY *CELL?*

OH, IT'S NOT SO BAD. YOU GET TO HANG OUT WITH *ME,* RIGHT?

OWW!

WHAT'S GOING **ON?**

THERE'S A *PROTOCOL!* WE'RE *INITIATING* IT!

I DIDN'T KNOW IT COULD DO *THAT...?*

WHAT ARE *THOSE?*

PART OF THE SECURITY PROTOCOL. YOU *ARE* A VISUAL AND AUDITORY *LEARNER,* RIGHT?

WHAT?

THAT'S HOW YOU *STORE* ALL THAT INFORMATION IN YOUR *HEAD,* RIGHT?

YEAH, BUT WHAT'S *THAT* GOT TO DO WITH --

I HAVE TO *DESTROY* THE MAINFRAME, AND I NEED YOU TO STORE THE *DATA.*

YOUR EYES WILL PROCESS THE *CONTENTS* OF THE MAINFRAME THROUGH THE LENSES AND INTO YOUR *BRAIN.*

I DON'T THINK I CAN *STORE* THAT MUCH INFORMATION.

YOU KNOW ALL THOSE *TESTS* THEY PUT YOU THROUGH? THEY KNOW *EXACTLY* WHAT YOU ARE CAPABLE OF. IF IT'S IN THE *PROTOCOL,* THAT MEANS YOU CAN *DO* IT.

BUT --

TRUST ME. I WOULDN'T *LIE* TO YOU.

HANA and DRUCKER'S PLOT DISCOVERED

R.D. HALL *Story* **TOM GRUMMETT** *Art*
CHRIS SOTOMAYOR *Colors* **COMICRAFT** *Lettering*

T.MONK ‹ENCRYPTED›:
They're destroying the mainframe.

K.APILA ‹ENCRYPTED›:
Drucker! What do we do?

T.MONK ‹ENCRYPTED›:
I'm afraid there is nothing we can do.

K.APILA ‹ENCR...
Phir Milengay Drucker.

THE END OF HANA and DRUCKER

R.D. HALL
Story

TOM GRUMMETT
Art

CHRIS SOTOMAYOR
Colors

COMICRAFT
Lettering

MATT, *WAKE UP!* COME **ON!**

MATT?

ELLE?

I KNEW YOU'D BE OKAY!

GREAT WORK, SON!

DID I DO OKAY?

YOU DID BETTER THAN OKAY! YOU SAVED THE DATA!

I DID IT FOR YOU.

YOU GUYS, I MEAN. I DID IT FOR YOU GUYS, BECAUSE YOU'VE DONE SO MUCH FOR ME.

I WANT YOU TO KNOW THAT I AM VERY PROUD OF YOU!

BOTH OF US, RIGHT, DADDY? I MEAN, I TOOK CARE OF DRUCKER AND GITELMAN, RIGHT?

YES, OF COURSE, SWEETHEART. CAN YOU SEE TO THE CLEAN UP WHILE I CONGRATULATE OUR YOUNG HERO?

HERO?

THAT'S RIGHT. AND I HAVE A SPECIAL TREAT IN STORE FOR YOU, YOUNG MAN.

KNOCK KNOCK KNOCK KNOCK

OH, NICE *DIGS*, DATABOY!

DON'T *BE* LIKE THAT.

WHATEVER -- IT'S JUST ANOTHER *CELL.*

THAT'S WHAT IT *IS!* LOOK!

I DON'T EVEN KNOW WHAT TIME OF *DAY* IT IS.

WHO *CARES* WHAT TIME OF DAY IT IS!

MAYBE *I* DO!

LOOK, AFTER THE DATA UPLOAD, I'VE ARRANGED A LITTLE *OUTSIDE* TIME. JUST ME AND YOU.

REALLY?

AND A GUARD, BUT IT'S *OUTSIDE.* SUNSHINE AND RAINBOWS AND ALL THAT CRAP, *RIGHT?*

I GUESS.

WE'RE *READY* FOR YOU NOW, MR. NEUENBERG.

The HISTORY of a SECRET

JOHN O'HARA and CARRI WAGNER *Story*   MICAH GUNNELL *Art*   MARK ROSLAN *Digital Inks* JOHN STARR *Colors*
COMICRAFT *Lettering*

FOR YEARS, ARCHAEOLOGISTS AND SCHOLARS HAVE WONDERED HOW THE EGYPTIANS BUILT THE PYRAMIDS.

IT IS ESTIMATED TO HAVE TAKEN HUNDREDS OF THOUSANDS OF MEN OVER 20 YEARS TO BUILD THE GREAT PYRAMID OF GIZA.

IT WAS AFTER THIS FIERCE BATTLE THAT TWO SAMURAI BEGAN FEUDING OVER THE SWORD OF ONI. EACH CLAIMED TO HAVE KILLED THIRTY-SEVEN WARRIORS OF THE ENEMY ARMY; AND THEREFORE, EACH CLAIMED THE BLADE AS A PRIZE FOR THEIR VALOR.

TAKEZO STEPPED BETWEEN THE TWO SAMURAI, FROWNING UPON THEIR SELFISH BEHAVIOR. *"YOU MAY WEAR THE UNIFORM OF THE SAMURAI, BUT YOU BICKER LIKE CHILDREN,"* KENSEI SAID.

"TRUE, EACH OF YOU FOUGHT VALIANTLY AGAINST THIS LATEST ENEMY TO JAPAN, BUT IN FIGHTING NOW WITH ONE ANOTHER, YOU DISHONOR YOURSELVES AND YOUR STANDING. USING YOUR LOGIC, THE SWORD SHOULD BELONG TO ME FOR I SLEW TWICE AS MANY ENEMIES AS EITHER OF YOU.

"BUT DOES THE SAMURAI WHO KILLS A HUNDRED ON THE BATTLEFIELD DESERVE MORE HONOR...MORE GLORY THAN THE BOY WHO SLAYS BUT ONE?

"IT IS ONLY TOGETHER THAT WE WIN. THERE IS NO INDIVIDUAL. THERE IS ONLY JAPAN."

SNAPPING THE BLADE WITH HIS OWN HANDS, KENSEI LEFT THE TWO SAMURAI EACH WITH HALF A BLADE...

...A REMINDER FOR THE REST OF THEIR DAYS OF HOW THEIR PRIDE HAD DAMAGED THEIR HONOR.

YOU SEE, *HIRO*, HOW THE GREAT TAKEZO KENSEI ALWAYS PUSHED FORWARD, NEVER SETTLING FOR FAILURE...IN HIMSELF OR IN OTHERS.

WHEN HE DIED, I WAS DEEPLY SADDENED BY THE LOSS.

BUT, I ALSO BELIEVED MY FATHER WAS HAPPIER NOW THAT HE COULD STAND BESIDE HIS HERO IN THE AFTERLIFE.

KIMIKO, PLEASE FORGIVE THE TIMING OF MY ADDRESS TO DISCUSS YAMAGATO INDUSTRIES, BUT THE BUSINESS WORLD STOPS FOR NO MAN...EVEN ONE AS GREAT AS YOUR FATHER.

KNOWING MY FATHER, *KIN,* I AM SURE HE WOULD ADMIRE YOUR DEDICATION TO HIS LEGACY. I KNOW WE HAVE MUCH WORK AHEAD OF US, AND I AM READY TO TAKE THE MANTLE.

ACTUALLY, KIMIKO, IT IS HIS LEGACY PROJECT THAT NOW SUFFERS FROM A LACK OF LEADERSHIP...

...THE *YAMAGATO FELLOWSHIP.*

219

MY FATHER'S INTENTIONS FOR MY ROLE AT YAMAGATO INDUSTRIES WERE CLEAR -- TO TAKE OVER THE POSITION THAT HE HELD...NOT TO BABYSIT HIS HOBBY.

YAMAGATO FELLOWSHIP

By looking into the past, it is our hope that we will be better equipped to identify and inspire the heroes walking among us today.

BUT THAT IS PRECISELY WHY THOSE WITHIN THE COMPANY HAVE SENT ME HERE -- TO DISTRACT MY ATTENTION WITH MY FATHER'S OBSESSION WHILE THEY WORK TO USURP MY RIGHTFUL PLACE IN HIS CHAIR.

WE ARE SO PLEASED TO HAVE YOU HERE WITH US, MS. NAKAMURA.

NOT AS PLEASED AS I AM. THANK YOU FOR RECEIVING ME ON SUCH SHORT NOTICE.

TELL ME, DAI. WHAT TIME DOES THE FACILITY OPEN?

UM... WE ARE OPEN.

I SEE.

WITHOUT MY FATHER PRAISING YOU, YOUR MEMORY APPEARS TO FALL ON DEAF EARS, KENSEI. IT SEEMS NOBODY ELSE IS INTERESTED IN YOU OR YOUR ADVENTURES.

PERHAPS IT IS TIME FOR YOU TO FIND A NEW HOME IN OBSCURITY.

EARLY 70s

THE WAR'S FINALLY OVER...

AT LEAST, FOR ME.

SOLDIERS WERE STARTING TO GO HOME... BUT NOT ME. I HAD NO HOME.

I DIDN'T KNOW WHERE TO BEGIN. I KNEW THERE WAS SOMETHING OUT THERE FOR ME, I JUST DIDN'T KNOW WHAT.

DRIVER'S WANTED

I TRIED TO FORGET ABOUT THE WAR...AND HOW LITTLE MY POWER ACTUALLY HELPED.

SOME THINGS YOU NEVER FORGET.

WHAT'S WAR LIKE?

HELL.

"LOST A LOT OF MY FRIENDS OUT THERE...

LOST A LOT OF MYSELF.

PLEASE, LET US GO.

I'LL GIVE YOU ANYTHING!

I AM HIS LIGHT.

GRIGSBY KIDNAPPED THE BUTLERS, A FAMILY OF FOUR, AND FOUND REFUGE IN THIS ABANDONED PLANTATION.

TIMES LIKE THIS, I THANK THAT EAGLE EYE.

I CAN MAKE IT AROUND HERE, BUT BARELY.

THUMP

CRAP...

HE WHO TRANSGRESSES MY WORD SHALL BE BLINDED...

I COULDN'T SEE A *THING.*

BUT I COULD *RUN* INTO WHERE I *SAW* HIM LAST.

HELP US.

PLEASE!

I NEEDED TO DO SOMETHING *NOW.* IF I *DIDN'T,* THIS FAMILY. THE HAITIAN. AND *I*...WOULDN'T *MAKE* IT.

MIGHT BE THE LAST *BULLET* I EVER *FIRED.*

LET'S SEE IF I CAN PUT MY *MONEY* WHERE MY *EYE CHART* IS.

KRA SH

233

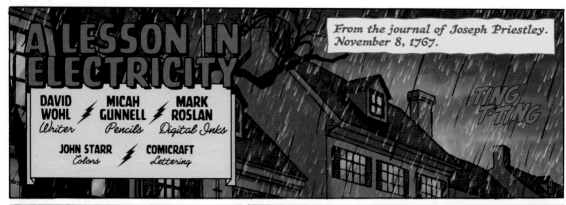

A LESSON IN ELECTRICITY

DAVID WOHL — Writer
MICAH GUNNELL — Pencils
MARK ROSLAN — Digital Inks
JOHN STARR — Colors
COMICRAFT — Lettering

From the journal of Joseph Priestley. November 8, 1767.

TING T-TING

It is with great apprehension that I write this entry...

NNNGGHHH... BENJAMIN....

TING TING TING

...but after several years of secrecy and consternation, I feel the truth must be explored.

BENJAMIN? THOSE INFERNAL BELLS OF YOURS ARE *RINGING* AGAIN! BEN?!

The truth about a colleague and dear friend of mine...

BEN! YOUR *BELLS!*

...Benjamin Franklin...

HNH? I--WHU--MY-- MY BELLS? WHAT DO YOU MEAN MY--

...And his famous experiment that changed our understanding of electricity forever.

MY *BELLS!*

CAN'T YOU INVENT A QUIETER WAY TO CONDUCT YOUR EXPER--

Although he was a sophisticated gentleman and world class statesman, Ben had a childlike curiosity about him.

FATHER? IS EVERYTHING ALL RIGHT?

THE BELLS ARE RINGING, WILL! ISN'T THAT *WONDERFUL?!*

He relished every small discovery, and, once he was interested, needed to thoroughly under~ stand anything and everything about a myriad of topics...

...including, in this case, *lightning*.

Contrary to the conventional wisdom of the day, Mr. Franklin believed that lightning was, in fact, made of electricity~and that it could be *controlled*.

To prove it, he first attached a large strip of iron to his roof and connected it to a series of bells.

This, he surmised, would alert him when there was lightning in the area.

Armed with this knowledge, he was determined to find a way to "capture" the lightning...

...thus proving that the so~called "Law of Conservation of Charge" applied to lightning.

MOTHER WISHES TO KNOW IF SHE CAN EXPECT YOU FOR BREAKFAST THIS MORNING.

But to do so, he was going to need some *help.*

AH, WILLIAM. I'M GLAD YOU'RE HERE. THERE'S SOMETHING I NEED TO SPEAK WITH YOU ABOUT...

Several days later, when he had the proper supplies and the weather conditions were favorable, they set out to conduct his experiment.

PLEASE HURRY, WILL. THERE ISN'T MUCH TIME!

GOOD AFTERNOON, MISTER FRANKLIN. I TRUST WHATEVER ACTIVITY YOU HAVE PLANNED FOR THIS AFTERNOON WILL BE QUIETER THAN THOSE BELLS THAT KEEP MY WIFE AND I UP FOR HALF THE NIGHT.

MY APOLOGIES, MR. BRADY. THEY SHAN'T BOTHER YOU MUCH LONGER. MY WORK IS NEARLY COMPLETE.

When Deborah asked where they were going on such a stormy day, Ben replied, simply...

...to fly a kite.

HMPH. WORK, INDEED.

WHAT A KOOK!

THIS IS A PERFECT SPOT.

To prove his thesis, Franklin realized that he needed to figure out a way to bring the lightning to him.

So, as everyone eventually learned, he chose a simple kite with a key attached to it.

The twine he attached to the kite was blended with metal, and it led to a jar at the bottom which would capture whatever electricity came down the wire.

To prevent electro-cution, he attached a dry silk string to the metal cord, effectively insulat-ing him from the charge of the key.

I DON'T THINK THAT WILL BE NECESSARY, WILLIAM. IT LOOKS LIKE THE SKY IS CLEARING EVERYWH--

Unfortunately there was one part of the process that he failed to consider.

DO YOU FEEL SOMETHING--?

FATHER?

SHOULD WE TRY TO FIND A DIFFERENT LOCATION, FATHER?

He never proposed the question, what if the dry string...was _wet_?

237

WHUMMMMMPPP

FATHER! FATHER! ARE YOU ALL RIGHT?

WE DID IT!

PLEASE LET ME HELP YOU UP.

NOT YET.

I BELIEVE SOME CHARGE IS STILL WITHIN ME.

COME HERE, TIGER.

THAT'S A GOOD BOY.

ZZZZZZT

WILL THAT HURT HIM?

NOT WITH ALL OF THAT FUR. HE'S WELL INSULATED.

Ironically, Benjamin had proven the Law of Conservation of Charge...on himself!

PIECES OF ME

J.T. KRUL *Story* **ROBERT ATKINS** *Art*

EDGAR @ STUDIO F *Colors*   **COMICRAFT** *Lettering*

IF *DREAMS* ARE A WAY FOR THE SUBCONSCIOUS TO SEND *MESSAGES* TO THE BRAIN, THEN MINE IS JUST PLAIN *NAGGING*, BECAUSE I HAVE THE SAME DREAM ALMOST *EVERY NIGHT*...

...THE SAME *TERRIBLE DREAM*.

YOU'RE *NEW*. BUT BEING PART OF THE DREAM, YOU *KNOW* THAT ALREADY, DON'T YOU?

HAVE YOU COME TO GIVE ME SOME *ANSWERS?* SOME *UNDERSTANDING?*

ONLY *YOU* HAVE THE ANSWER. LIFE IS TO BE *UNDERSTOOD*, IT IS NOTHING TO BE FEARED.

GREAT. I DIDN'T *THINK* SO.

AND, AGAIN WE HAVE CROWS... ALWAYS *SEVEN*. AND HERE I THOUGHT THAT WAS SUPPOSED TO BE A *LUCKY* NUMBER.

WHAT DO *YOU* THINK?

OH, SO IT'S GOING TO BE LIKE *THAT*, HUH?

LIKE I SAID, I'VE HAD THIS DREAM BEFORE. BUT STILL, EACH TIME IT FEELS *NEW*.

HEARING MY OWN NAME *ALWAYS* STARTLES ME.

RYAN...

IT SOUNDS LIKE IT'S COMING FROM THE TOP OF THE STAIRS.

RYAN...

RYAN...

BUT THE HIGHER I CLIMB, THE *SOFTER* THE VOICE BECOMES.

RYAN...

AND THEN...IT'S *GONE*.

241

RYAN... THIS IS YOUR LIFE. *PARTS* OF IT, ANYWAY.

THE GOOD, THE BAD, AND EVEN THE *UGLY*.

THE IMAGES MAKE MY BLOOD BOIL. I WANT TO DRIVE MY FIST THROUGH THE GLASS... *ERASE* IT FROM MY MEMORY. IT HURTS TOO MUCH TO REMEMBER HOW SHE LEFT... HOW SHE WAS *TAKEN* FROM ME.

THIS TIME, I *UNDERSTAND*.

THAT'S STRANGE.

IS THAT ME?

WHAT ARE YOU SMILING AT?

HEY!

...WHILE YOU DIRECT YOUR ATTENTION *ELSEWHERE.*

FOCUS ON WHAT MATTERS *MOST*...

...THE *LIFE* YOU STILL *HAVE.*

END

THE CORINTHIAN CASINO.

OVER TWO MILLION SQUARE FEET OF CONCRETE, STEEL, ITALIAN MARBLE, SLOT MACHINES, CHROME BIDETS AND IN-ROOM MOVIE THEATERS.

Live from Las Vegas

THE BRAINCHILD OF ENTREPRENEUR DANIEL LINDERMAN, IT'S A SPRAWLING MONUMENT TO *EXCESS.*

AND THAT FITS LINDERMAN *PERFECTLY.*

LINDERMAN WAS MY BOSS, THOUGH TO THIS DAY, I'M NOT EXACTLY SURE HOW HE FOUND ME IN THE FIRST PLACE.

I WAS FRESH OUT OF COLLEGE, STRUGGLING TO EARN A LIVING, TOILING AT A FEW MEANINGLESS I.T. JOBS.

THEN, OUT OF NOWHERE, I GOT THE CALL.

DANIEL LINDERMAN WANTED TO MEET ME.

ON THE LAM

DAVID WOHL *Writer* **ERIC NGUYEN** *Art* **SHADEDGREY PRODUCTIONS** *Colors* **COMICRAFT** *Lettering*

...UNTIL HE ASKED ME TO DO A "FAVOR" FOR A FRIEND -- A NEW YORK POLITICIAN NAMED *NATHAN PETRELLI*.

MY JOB WAS TO HELP PETRELLI GET ELECTED, WITH A LITTLE ASSISTANCE FROM SOME OTHER PROGRAMMERS AND AN UNSUSPECTING NEW YORK ELECTION OFFICIAL.

SINCE THE VOTING MACHINES WERE OWNED BY LINDERMAN, IT WASN'T DIFFICULT TO DOCTOR THE RESULTS WITH A PIECE OF SOFTWARE CALLED A *LOGIC BOMB*.

PROBLEM WAS... WE GOT HACKED.

WITH THE ELECTION SUDDENLY IN SHAMBLES, LINDERMAN WAS LIVID.

I'D HEARD STORIES ABOUT WHAT HAPPENED TO GUYS WHO ENDED UP ON HIS BAD SIDE...

...AND SINCE I HAD NO INTENTION OF JOINING THEM AT THE BOTTOM OF LAKE MEAD, I TOOK OFF.

WITH THE HELP OF SOME CONNECTIONS I PICKED UP OVER THE YEARS, I CREATED A NEW IDENTITY FOR MYSELF AND WAS ABLE TO SLIP THROUGH THE CRACKS.

...AND THE DAYS WERE ALL THE SAME.

NOW I LIVE HERE, IN AN ABANDONED NUCLEAR FALLOUT SHELTER.

WHEN I TELL PEOPLE, THEY THINK I'M BEING TRENDY. BUT I'M REALLY JUST BROKE.

RUNNING FROM LINDERMAN COST ME EVERYTHING...

...BUT AT LEAST I'M STILL ALIVE.

UNLIKE LINDERMAN.

Live from Las Vegas

TOO MANY ENEMIES, I GUESS.

AND AS THE LAST VESTIGES OF HIS EMPIRE CRUMBLE TO THE GROUND, I REALIZE THAT IT'S TIME FOR ME TO COME OUT OF THE SHADOWS.

www.brianundaunted.

...I realize that it's time for me to come out of the shadows.

www.brianundaunted.

It's time for me to start asking questions: who ruined my life, and **why**

It's time for me...to get **even.**

IT'S TIME FOR ME... TO GET *EVEN.*

IT'S TIME FOR ME TO START ASKING QUESTIONS: WHO RUINED MY LIFE, AND *WHY?*

1972

YOU'RE *OUTTA* HERE, TAVARA!

I DON'T GET IT, RONDO. WHAT'S UP WITH YOU?

BOUNTY HUNTER

| **R.D. HALL** | **ROBERT ATKINS** | **EDGAR @ STUDIO F** | **COMICRAFT** |
| *Writer* | *Art* | *Colors* | *Lettering* |

YOU'RE A REAL LOOKER, AND YOU'RE PART BLOODHOUND WHEN IT COMES TO TRACKING DOWN MARKS, BUT I GOTTA--

THAT'S RIGHT, I DO MY JOB AND I DO IT WELL. I DON'T SEE THE *PROBLEM.*

IT'S THE ONES YOU DON'T FIND. THAT'S THE PROBLEM. *NO ONE* FINDS THEM. AT LEAST, NOT ALIVE ANYWAYS.

YOU GOT SOMETHING YOU WANT TO SAY TO ME, RONDO? BECAUSE IF YOU DO...

YOU CAN JUST SPIT IT OUT, RIGHT NOW!

LOOK, TAVARA, YOU'RE A GOOD KID. AND I'M NOT ACCUSING *YOU* OF ANYTHING. I JUST CAN'T HANDLE THIS KINDA HEAT FROM THE COPS RIGHT NOW. I'M SORRY.

THE COPS?

I'LL GET MY THINGS.

ONE WEEK LATER.

YES MA'AM, HE'S WITH ME NOW. I CAN HAVE HIM AT THE RENDEZVOUS POINT TOMORROW.

THREE WEEKS LATER.

YOU'LL LIKE THE EVALUATORS, PAMELA. THEY'RE VERY NICE, AND THEY CAN'T *WAIT* TO MEET YOU.

FOUR WEEKS LATER.

NO, I'M SORRY, MA'AM, THE WAITRESS SAID JASON WELKES *QUIT* THREE WEEKS AGO.

YES, I'M SORRY TOO.

WHAT CAN I GET YOU, PRETTY LADY?

I'M LOOKING FOR JASON WELKES. YOU SEEN HIM?

ONLY EVERY TIME I LOOK IN THE MIRROR.

THEN YOU'RE JUST THE MAN I'M LOOKING FOR.

255

CONGRATULATIONS, YOU CLOSED DOWN THE BAR.

I AM SOOOO *TRASHED!*

SINCE WE'RE THE LAST ONES TO LEAVE, I'LL DRIVE YOU HOME. WHERE DO YOU LIVE?

WAIT, WAIT, I GOTTA GET SOMETHING OUT OF MY CAR FIRST!

WHOA, HOLD ON!

COME ON! IT'S IN THE TRUNK!

SO WHAT WAS IT THAT YOU WANTED TO SHOW ME...?

I DON'T SEE ANYTHING.

JUST A LITTLE SOMETHING TO REMEMBER YOU BY.

TWO FOR THEM, ONE FOR *ME.* THAT'S SEEMS FAIR.

PLEASE GET IN, LINDA, BEFORE YOU CATCH YOUR *DEATH* OUT THERE.

THIS IS A DOSSIER ON YOUR NEXT ACQUISITION. HE'LL BE ARRIVING IN DENVER FRIDAY AFTERNOON.

WOW, HIGH FUNCTIONING. THIS SHOULD BE FUN.

YES, AND I WANT THIS ONE BROUGHT DIRECTLY TO ME.

SPEAKING OF WHICH, WHY HAVE YOU BEEN OUT OF CONTACT?

I'M SORRY, *SOMETHING* CAME UP.

DO YOU HAVE A LEAD ON JASON WELKES YET?

NO, NOTHING. I THINK YOUR INTEL MAY HAVE BEEN WRONG.

THAT'S NOT LIKELY. DID YOU ASK HIS FRIENDS? FAMILY? HAS *ANYONE* SEEN HIM?

NO. NOT IN WEEKS, LIKE I SAID ON THE PHONE.

THEN PERHAPS YOU'RE NOT THE RIGHT WOMAN FOR THIS OPERATION. I CAN'T AFFORD YOU BOTCHING THIS NEXT ACQUISITION.

WHAT? *NO!*

I'M SORRY, MISS TAVARA.

I *PANICKED*, I COULDN'T LET HER TAKE HIM AWAY FROM ME.

POWERS OR NOT, SHE HAD TO *DIE*.

WELCOME TO CENTENNIAL AIRPORT IN *BEAUTIFUL* DENVER, COLORADO. WE HOPE YOU ENJOY YOUR STAY.

Daniel Linderman, arriving gate 7, Friday, 3:00 P.M.

ZONED OUT...OVER MEDICATED...STONED.

THAT'S WHAT EVERYONE KEEPS SAYING BEHIND MY BACK.

NOBODY SAYS IT TO MY FACE. NOT THAT I WOULD NOTICE EVEN IF THEY DID.

GUESS THAT'S WHAT HAPPENS WHEN YOU'VE BEEN REDUCED TO BEING A ZOMBIE.

BUT IT HAS NOTHING TO DO WITH DRUGS OR ALCOHOL.

PSYCHIC BOUNDS

J.T. KRUL
Writer

MICAH GUNNEL
Pencils

MARK ROSLAN
Digital Inks

JOHN STARR
Colors

COMICRAFT
Lettering

DEBBIE!

IT'S OKAY, PIPER. IT'S ALL OKAY.

I...I REMEMBER NOW.

THERE WAS NOTHING EXTRATERRESTRIAL ABOUT MY ABDUCTION THAT NIGHT.

THOSE MEN VIOLATED MY BODY AND MY MIND BEFORE SOMEHOW ERASING THE ENTIRE EVENT FROM MY MEMORY.

OR, I SHOULD SAY, OUR MEMORY. BECAUSE NOW I KNOW THE TRUTH...SHE ISN'T FROM MY DREAMS. DEBBIE IS FROM MY PAST.

I HAVE A SISTER.

DOCTOR, SHE'S HAVING THE DREAMS AGAIN. THE DELUSIONS OF A SISTER... SHE SEEMED SO GOOD FOR SO LONG. I DON'T UNDERSTAND WHAT HAPPENED.

IT'S OKAY. SOMETIMES EXTERNAL FORCES TRIGGER THE EPISODES. YOU DID THE RIGHT THING BY CALLING.

DON'T WORRY, WE'LL BE RIGHT OVER...

END

264

LINDA TAVARA, 1967

My parents are afraid of me. I can tell.

KNOCK KNOCK

YES?

IS EVERYTHING OKAY, HONEY?

I'M FINE, MOM.

WE'RE JUST DOWN THE HALL IF YOU NEED ANYTHING, SWEETHEART, OKAY?

I SAID I'M FINE! REALLY.

They won't even come into my room anymore.

That's just as well. I don't want them to come into my room and see what's in the boxes.

Ground Squirrel: Backyard

Linda's Journal

There had to be more to life than my tiny house, my tiny room, and my tiny back yard-- filled with tiny animals with tiny auras. Auras, I guess that's what you call them.

Ground Squirrel Backyard

I wanted more.

I dream about auras every night. Lots of them.

They wait for me. It's like each person holds a star beneath their skin, each one begging to escape.

Some of them shine so bright I couldn't help but be warmed by their presence.

I longed for that warmth. And, with every touch of every hand, I felt it flow through me.

I could feel everything, their hopes, their dreams for the future, while they no longer felt anything at all. Their spark belonged to me now.

Whenever I had those dreams I awoke with an intense craving to feel the way I felt in my dreams.

One night, I couldn't stand the gnawing thirst any longer.

I spent my nights just watching others--observing the beautiful colors that surrounded them.

Some beamed bright like beacons.

Others flickered like tiny candles.

But they all called out to me. Begging me to take them.

I stalked the streets, night after night. Looking for something, I just didn't know what.

RETIREM
VILL

Until I saw her light.

ANGELS!

Her light wasn't just bright, it blazed.

YOU DON'T KNOW NOTHING ABOUT NO ANGELS, IDA MAY WALKER!

I'VE SEEN 'EM, WHEN I WAS A LITTLE GIRL. THEY WOULD COME TO ME.

THEN HOW COME I'VE NEVER SEEN ONE?

I had to make her light mine.

MAYBE THEY DON'T WANT YOU TO SEE THEM BECAUSE YOU'RE SUCH A SOURPUSS!

MAYBE YOU'RE A NUT!

DO YOU NEED A VISITOR'S PASS, MISS?

WHAT? OH, YES.

VISITOR

268

SAID YOU HAVE A TELEPHONE CALL IN YOUR ROOM.

A TELEPHONE CALL? FOR ME?

MAYBE IT'S ONE OF THEM ANGELS.

YOU JUST BE QUIET, YOU OLD SOW! AND DON'T YOU CHEAT WHILE I'M GONE, EITHER!

She really was a sweet old woman.

THAT MEAN OLD BIDDY, I DON'T EVEN KNOW WHY I PLAY DOMINOES WITH HER.

YES, MA'AM.

I WONDER WHO WOULD BE CALLING ME AT THIS HOUR?

HELLO? HELLO? THERE'S NO ONE THERE.

I KNOW, MA'AM. I'M SORRY I LIED TO YOU.

I DON'T UNDERSTAND? WHAT DO YOU WANT?

As bad as I wanted her light, I just couldn't lie to her anymore.

I CAME HERE FOR YOU.

FOR ME? ARE YOU? ARE YOU AN ANGEL?

Okay, I lied a little.

AN ANGEL?

YES, MY DEAR, OF COURSE I AM.

It was just like my dreams. The heat traveled up my fingers and into my chest, filling me with white, loving light.

And something else.

Now I could see Ida's angels as well.

CALL AN AMBULANCE! IDA WALKER'S STOPPED BREATHING!

MOONLIGHT SERENADE

R. D. HALL
Writer

JASON BADOWER
Art

ANNETTE KWOK
Colors

COMICRAFT
Lettering

270